Collaborating Online

Collaborating Online

Learning Together in Community

Rena M. Palloff

Keith Pratt

JOSSEY-BASS
A Wiley Imprint
www.josseybass.com

Library of Congress Cataloging-in-Publication Data

Palloff, Rena M., 1950–
    Collaborating online : learning together in community / Rena M. Palloff, Keith Pratt.— 1st ed.
        p. cm.
    Includes bibliographical references and index.
    ISBN 0-7879-7614-8 (alk. paper)
    1. Group work in education. 2. Computer-assisted instruction. I. Pratt, Keith, 1947- II. Title.
    LB1032.P334 2005
    371.39'5'0285—dc22   2004017931

Contents

Preface

*C**ollaboration.* This is a word that sends chills up the spines of some instructors. For them, collaboration brings visions of students who resist working in groups, the struggle to create equitable teams of students, uneven participation, and the difficulty of evaluating and grading the products produced by a group. For others, however, collaboration can be an exciting adventure. For these instructors, collaboration means sending students off to work together in creative ways, moving out of the box of traditional papers and projects, and empowering students to deepen the learning experience through their work with one another.

In the online environment, collaboration can be seen as the cornerstone of the educational experience. Just about everything that students engage in online, from participation on a discussion board to working in small groups, can be viewed as collaborative. In our previous work (Palloff and Pratt, 1999, 2001, 2003), we have noted that collaboration forms the foundation of a learning community online—it brings students together to support the learning of each member of the group while promoting creativity and critical thinking.

A recent conversation with an instructional designer provided the impetus to devote a book to the topic of collaboration and its connection with online learning communities. He said, "I've just read *Building Learning Communities in Cyberspace* (Palloff and Pratt, 1999) and *Online Communities* (Preece, 2000). I now get the concepts behind community building online, but I still don't know how exactly to *do* it. Can you help me with that?" This conversation is not unlike others we have had with faculty across the United States and Canada as we have made presentations to them about online learning communities—faculty get the concepts, but need assistance with the "how" of building community and making collaboration happen. This book is intended as a guide to doing just that. It provides some basic concepts involved in understanding collaboration and community building, followed by concrete suggestions and activities that make it happen.

AUDIENCE

The audience for this book is clearly faculty who are teaching online or who are venturing into the online arena for the first time. In addition, it is intended for those who are designing and developing courses so that they can create collaborative activities that are effective and successful. Instructional designers will benefit from this work in that they will be better able to support faculty in carrying out collaborative activities online. Although not specifically intended for a corporate audience, the book will also assist those engaged in training in the corporate arena and will provide ideas for the inclusion of collaborative work in training employees. Faculty developers will find the book useful as well in the development of collaborative training programs for faculty.

ORGANIZATION

This book is intended as a guide or handbook for implementing collaborative activity in online classes. Therefore, the theoretical material has been kept to a minimum and the organization of the book is slightly different from that of our previous work. Part One is devoted to presenting the theory behind collaboration and collaborative activity in an online course. Chapter One reviews some basic theory about collaboration, online collaboration, and working with virtual teams. Chapter Two discusses the process of online collaboration—where do we start and how do we make it happen? Chapter Three looks at the challenges instructors may face when implementing collaborative activity online, from groups that refuse to work with one another to issues surrounding assessment of collaborative work. Chapter Four provides a discussion of the important and frequently frustrating topic of evaluation of collaborative activity and student assessment when collaboration is used.

Part Two contains a number of ideas for collaborative activities, with suggestions for using them in an online course. These certainly do not represent every collaborative activity possible, but give the reader a selection of activities that have proven to be successful online and are designed to trigger the imagination. Further application of these activities is encouraged, as well as the development of other activities based on the ideas presented here. As with our previous books, we pepper these discussions with quotes from our students and from other faculty who have worked with us in the development of these ideas and techniques; we are very grateful to all of them for their contribution to our ongoing work.

THE SERIES

We are excited to present this book as one of a series of guides for faculty who teach online. We have been privileged to work as the consulting editors on this series and are pleased to be adding our contribution to those of our esteemed colleagues in the world of online learning. It is our hope that faculty who teach online will find these books to be valuable desk references that are used often as they design and facilitate online courses.

ACKNOWLEDGMENTS

There are a number of people we would like to thank for their assistance with this work. First, our editor, David Brightman, who originated the idea for this series, hired us as consulting editors for it, and suggested that we make a contribution to it sooner rather than later. We would also like to thank our production editor, Cathy Mallon, for her patience and her support of us in all of our work. Our thanks to Dean Janoff, our colleague from the Fielding Graduate Institute, who gave us the idea for the title of this work. Additional thanks go to Diana Dell and A. J. Styer, two of our learners who generously contributed pieces of their own work, and to our faculty colleague and friend, Cheryl Doran, who did the same. We also extend thanks to all of our students at the Fielding Graduate Institute and at Capella University—your comments and contributions to our online classes have triggered many of the thoughts and concepts that we present here. We thank Rita-Marie Conrad and Cyd Strickland for their friendship, support, and all the great conversations. Finally, we thank our families for their endless support, patience, and love.

Rena M. Palloff   Keith Pratt
Alameda, California   Bella Vista, Arkansas

About the Authors

Rena Palloff and Keith Pratt are managing partners of Crossroads Consulting Group, working with institutions, organizations, and corporations interested in the development of online distance learning and training programs.

Rena and Keith are the authors of the 1999 Frandson Award-winning book, *Building Learning Communities in Cyberspace* (Jossey-Bass, 1999), *Lessons from the Cyberspace Classroom* (Jossey-Bass, 2001), and *The Virtual Student* (Jossey-Bass, 2003). The books are comprehensive guides to the development of an online environment that helps promote successful learning outcomes while building and fostering a sense of community among the learners. Drs. Palloff and Pratt have been presenting this work across the United States and internationally since 1994, as well as consulting to academic institutions regarding the development of effective distance learning programs.

Rena M. Palloff has consulted extensively in health care, academic settings, and addiction treatment for well over twenty years. Rena is faculty at the Fielding Graduate Institute, in both the Educational Leadership and Change Program and the master's degree program in Organizational Management/Organization Development. She is also adjunct faculty at Capella University in the School of Human Services. In addition, she has taught classes on organizational behavior and management and leadership on an adjunct basis for the International Studies Program at Ottawa University in Ottawa, Kansas, in various sites throughout the Pacific Rim. Rena received a bachelor's degree in sociology from the University of Wisconsin-Madison and a master's degree in social work from the University of Wisconsin-Milwaukee. She holds a master's degree in organizational development and a Ph.D. in human and organizational systems from the Fielding Graduate Institute.

Keith Pratt began his government career as a computer systems technician with the Air Force in 1967. After leaving the Air Force, Keith held positions as registrar and faculty at Charter College, director at Chapman College, and trainer and consultant at The Growth Company. Keith was an assistant professor in the International Studies Program and the chair of the Management Information Systems Program, main campus and overseas, at Ottawa University in Ottawa, Kansas. Keith is currently adjunct faculty at the Fielding Graduate Institute in educational leadership and change as well as at a number of other institutions, including Baker University and Northwest Arkansas Community College. He has served as a senior project manager for Datatel, working with community colleges throughout the United States and Canada on administrative software installations. Keith graduated from Wayland Baptist University with a dual degree in business administration and computer systems technology. He has a master of science degree in human resource management (with honors) from Chapman University. He holds a master's degree in organizational development and a Ph.D. in human and organizational systems from the Fielding Graduate Institute and an honorary doctorate of science in economics from Moscow State University.

Collaboration Online

Collaboration in the Online Environment

Collaboration Basics

Online instructors cannot deliver knowledge;
online learners must seek it out.

Styers, 2004, p. 61.

The first wave of online instruction appears to have crested. During that first wave, instructors who were considered early adopters of the technology involved with online teaching experimented with course designs that would move their instruction into that arena. They experienced both successes and failures as they tried new approaches and techniques for engaging learners online. The second wave, which is concerned with best practices and improving both interaction and interactivity in online courses, is upon us. We now make distinctions between interaction and interactivity—*interaction* referring to the all-important student-to-student and student-to-instructor contact that has become the hallmark of online learning; *interactivity* meaning the inclusion of material that helps to create active learning online, such as the use of multimedia in courses. "Read and discuss" online classes are no longer seen as the best way to deliver content.

We also see online instructors continuously searching for ways to improve student-to-student interaction in their courses, to create more personal and relevant learning experiences, and to promote the development of active and engaged learners. Today's online instructor recognizes the value of collaboration online but may not have all the tools available to make it happen successfully.

In their seminal work, *Joining Together,* Johnson and Johnson (2000) write about positive group interdependence, which they state exists "when one perceives that one is linked with others in a way so that one cannot succeed unless they do (and vice versa) and/or that one must coordinate one's efforts with the efforts of others to complete a task." In other words, they state, group members "sink or swim together" (p. 115). Through this definition, Johnson and Johnson aptly describe the very foundation of collaboration—when I succeed, we succeed. Srinivas (n.d.) defines collaboration as "an educational approach to teaching and learning that involves groups of learners working together to solve a problem, complete a task, or create a product" (¶ 1). We have previously noted (2003) that collaborative activity is important in both face-to-face and online classes because it promotes the following:

- Development of critical thinking skills
- Co-creation of knowledge and meaning
- Reflection
- Transformative learning (Palloff and Pratt, pp. 35–37)

Johnson and Johnson are indicating that a sense of community, as we have defined it in our previous work (Palloff and Pratt, 1999), needs to exist in order for collaboration to occur. We believe, however, that collaborative activity can also help to develop that sense of community, thus enabling the creation of an environment in which further collaborative work can happen. Figure 1.1 illustrates the cyclical nature of this relationship—collaboration supports the creation of community and community supports the ability to collaborate.

Srinivas's definition tells us what collaboration looks like in practice and incorporates the notion that the teaching process is included here as well—it is not just the learners who collaborate with one another under instructor guidance, the instructor is a part of that collaborative process as well. In our experience, this process occurs in numerous ways, from the way in which the instructor sets the stage for collaborative activity to the ways in which the activities are evaluated and evaluation data are used to develop collaborative work further. This inclusiveness supports our notion that the instructor is an important member of the learning community, helping to form and shape it and empowering learners to take on the responsibility to nurture it, extend it, and use it as the vehicle for co-created knowledge and meaning.

Figure 1.1. The Cycle of Community and Collaboration.

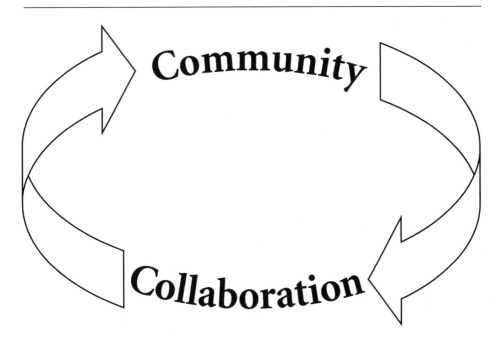

In this first chapter, we briefly review theoretical material about collaboration. We then discuss the importance of collaboration online and begin to set the stage for working with virtual groups or teams in online classes. This more theoretical chapter will set the stage for the more practical information to follow in the balance of the book.

COLLABORATION—THE HALLMARK OF CONSTRUCTIVISM

Collaboration has often been defined as the "heart and soul" of an online course or, for that matter, any course that bases its theoretical foundation in constructivism. The theory of constructivism, first attributed to Piaget (1969), holds that the process of learning is active and is involved with constructing rather than acquiring knowledge. The theory further notes that individuals learn through interaction with their world and that they develop knowledge through social interaction rather than individual exploration. Jonassen and others (1995) note that the collaboration in a constructivist classroom results not only in personal meaning-making on the part of the individual student, but also creates a container wherein social construction of knowledge and meaning can occur. Brookfield (1995) contends that collaborative processes promote initiative, creativity, critical thinking skills, and dialogue on the part of the learners. Collaboration, then, accomplishes a number of outcomes:

• *Assists with deeper levels of knowledge generation.* When online classes are developed from a collaborative framework, the central theme is the co-construction of knowledge and meaning. When working in small groups, teams, or even on the discussion board of an online course, the ability to create knowledge and meaning is enhanced.

• *Promotes initiative, creativity, and critical thinking.* In his discussion of critical thinking, Stephen Brookfield (1987) notes, "Critical thinking is complex and frequently perplexing since it requires the suspension of belief and the jettisoning of assumptions previously accepted without question. As people strive for clarity in self-understanding, and as they try to change aspects of their lives, the opportunity to discuss these activities is enormously helpful" (p. 10). Thus, the ability to collaborate enables the development of the ability to think critically, a skill that is more difficult to master individually.

• *Allows students to create a shared goal for learning and forms the foundation of a learning community.* In our previous work, we have noted that a learning community is the vehicle through which learning occurs in the online course (Palloff and Pratt, 1999, 2001, 2003). Beginning an online course with a discussion of learning objectives and working toward a common goal not only creates the foundation of that learning community, it is also the first step toward collaboration. If students are clear from the beginning of the course that "we're all in this together," then incorporating collaborative activity into the course happens much more easily.

• *Addresses all learning styles.* When an online course is developed using the concept of learning cycles—a systematic set of activities that build on each other and scaffold learning, collaborative projects, or complex activities that demand that students use multiple skills—all learning styles are tapped. Consequently, in using collaborative approaches to learning, the instructor can be assured that the various learning preferences in the group will be addressed and that the less preferred styles may be further developed.

• *Addresses issues of culture.* Collaborative activity enables students to construct their own knowledge and apply prior experience and their own culturally preferred ways of knowing to the task. Consequently, through collaboration, it is likely that a more culturally sensitive online classroom can be created.

Although these concepts are being applied to online learning, collaboration serves the same functions in face-to-face or blended (also known as hybrid) classes as well. Collaboration assists the instructor and all students in successfully achieving learning objectives more easily. Although collaboration takes more time, the outcome is actually a deeper, more efficient, and complete learning process.

WHY COLLABORATE ONLINE?

The online environment can be a lonely place. Students and faculty alike report feelings of isolation when working online. The benefits of taking or teaching an online class—being able to connect any time and any place, from one's bedroom in pajamas and bunny slippers or from a library or computer lab—also can be a detriment of sorts given that, for the most part, the people with whom one is interacting are represented by words on a screen.

Recent studies of the online learning environment have noted that involvement or "social presence," better known as a feeling of community and connection among learners, has contributed positively to learning outcomes and learner satisfaction with online courses. Tu and Corry (2002) identified three dimensions of social presence: social context, online communication, and interaction. Picciano (2002) found a consistently strong relationship among learner perceptions of interaction, social presence, and learning. Gunawardena and Zittle (1997) linked social presence to student satisfaction with online courses. Kazmer (2000) noted that building a learning community is necessary for a sense of social presence and, ultimately, for successful learner-to-learner interaction. In an earlier study, Murphy, Drabier, and Epps (1998) noted that the use of asynchronous online collaboration increased learner interaction, satisfaction, and learning.

Beyond learner satisfaction, however, is the more important belief that collaboration enhances learning outcomes and reduces the potential for learner isolation that can occur in the online environment. By learning together in a learning community, students have the opportunity to extend and deepen their learning experience, test out new ideas by sharing them with a supportive group, and receive critical and constructive feedback. The likelihood of successful achievement of learning objectives and achieving course competencies increases through collaborative engagement. Conrad and Donaldson (2004) state, "[The] collaborative acquisition of knowledge is one key to the success of creating an online learning environment. Activities that require student interaction and encourage a sharing of ideas promote a deeper level of thought" (p. 5). Figure 1.2 depicts our model of online collaboration built around the notions of social presence, constructivism, and the use of an online learning community to achieve successful outcomes in an online course.

The advancing study of online community informs us that community is made up of more than what we originally thought. The elements of community, as we previously identified them (Palloff and Pratt, 1999 and 2003) included the following:

- *People:* The students, faculty, and staff involved in an online course
- *Shared purpose:* Coming together to take an online course, including sharing information, interests, and resources
- *Guidelines:* Create the structure for the online course, by providing the ground rules for interaction and participation
- *Technology:* The vehicle for delivery of the course and a place where everyone involved can meet
- *Collaborative learning:* Student-to-student interaction that also supports socially constructed meaning and creation of knowledge
- *Reflective practice:* Promoting transformative learning

Figure 1.2. Model of Online Collaboration.

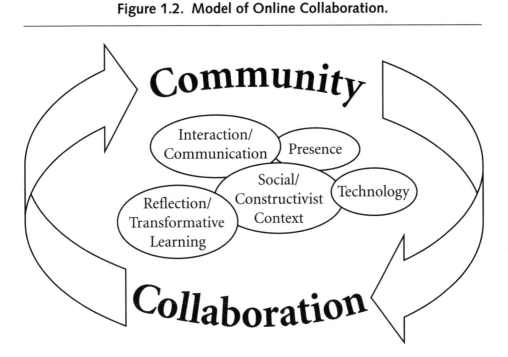

We now note that social presence is a critical element of the online community and one that is critical to collaborative work. As we move through this book, we will refer back to this model as a driving force in the development of our concepts and ideas around the important role that collaboration plays in an online course.

COLLABORATION ONLINE

Very few guidelines currently exist for collaboration in the online environment, although there is a great deal of interest surrounding the idea. There are numerous ways in which an instructor can create collaboration online, regardless of the content area being studied. Some suggestions include the following:

- Small-group assignments
- Research assignments asking students to seek out and present additional resource material to their peers

- Group work on case studies

- Simulations

- Shared facilitation

- Homework forums

- Asynchronous discussion of the reading and discussion questions

- Papers posted to the course site with mutual feedback provided

In Part Two, we review these and other forms of collaborative activity that might be included in an online course, with specific examples for how to carry out each activity and tips for assessment. At this juncture, however, it is important to look at how the specific activities lend themselves to creating the sense of social presence and the learning community through which learning happens.

All of these activities demand a sense of social presence and community in order to be successful—students and faculty alike need to interact and communicate frequently as collaborative work ensues. There needs to be a sense of shared responsibility for learning. The greatest complaint about collaborative work from both instructors and students is the uneven participation of group members. Many of the activities listed cannot be done in isolation; for example, work on small-group projects or participation in a simulation that involves taking roles are activities that demand equal participation across the group. Although uneven involvement might be less of an issue with activities such as sharing research findings or rotated facilitation, it still presents a source of frustration for students and instructors when presence is not there. In Chapter Three, we discuss collaboration challenges, including the lack of presence, along with suggestions for intervention.

Regardless of how collaborative activity is used online, the instructor is responsible for creating the container through which it can happen effectively. Consequently, the instructor needs to set the stage for collaborative activity by focusing on the development of a learning community and creating the environment for collaboration by encouraging collaborative activity from the first day of the course and explaining and modeling its importance. In the next chapter, we focus more closely on the process of collaboration and how the instructor can be effective in each stage of the process, thereby increasing social presence and reducing the likelihood of uneven participation.

WORKING WITH VIRTUAL TEAMS

The business world has recently contributed to our knowledge of collaboration through an emphasis on virtual teaming. The resulting body of literature can assist the academic world in understanding how distributed teams work and how collaboration is possible at a distance. The use of teamwork in an online class can, in addition to assisting with knowledge generation, prepare today's learners for today's work world. Duarte and Snyder (2001) note, "Understanding how to work in or lead a virtual team is becoming a fundamental competence for people in many organizations. . . . It is not uncommon to talk with people who lead or work in virtual teams who do not have a great deal of experience working on teams in a co-located environment. . . . People who lead and work in virtual teams need to have special skills, including an understanding of human dynamics, knowledge of how to manage across functional areas and national cultures, and the ability to use communication technologies as their primary means of communicating and collaborating" (p. 4). The inclusion of collaborative group work in an online class can help to develop the skills that will be needed to lead or function in a virtual team in the work environment, particularly if learners are encouraged to reflect on the potential application of these skills.

Duarte and Snyder further describe the seven competencies that they believe are critical to the successful leadership of virtual teams. Some of these competencies might be considered skills that the instructor of the online course needs to have, but others are skills that learners would need to have or to develop as they work in virtual teams in their online classes. They are the following:

Performance Coaching and Management

Included in this category of competence are activities at the team level that can assist the team with completing its work. The activities are similar to those included in the development of a team charter, which we address in the next chapter. In brief, they include developing the team's vision, mission, and strategy; negotiating the accountability of each member; identifying results and deliverables; developing methods to review progress and results; and sharing best practices with other teams. It is not necessarily the instructor's responsibility to actually do all of these jobs; instead, the instructor empowers the team to take on these functions. The instructor, however, may act as a coach to ensure that collaborative activity flows smoothly.

Appropriate Use of Technology

Often in an educational situation, the available technology is the course-management system in use, although there are now numerous asynchronous and synchronous technologies that can assist with facilitation of collaborative work. The instructor should consider the needs of the team when recommending or determining which forms of technology will be used for a collaborative activity. As an example, one of us was teaching a course where students were asked to form teams to work in a coaching situation to explore the use of self in organizational consulting. One team decided to subdivide into dyads to complete the activity that would then report the results back to their team. The team requested the option of going outside of the course-management system to use phone contact and instant messaging to complete their work. This permission was granted, with the stipulation that the results of each contact be posted to the course so that others would have the opportunity to follow the process of the dyads. The result was a deep and rich learning experience for everyone.

Cross-Cultural Management

When groups are made up of learners who span the globe and who live in other countries and cultures, it is the responsibility of the instructor to make sure that there is cultural sensitivity among group members. Some initial exploration of this topic before a group is asked to do its collaborative work is often enough, coupled with a discussion of the implications for the team. For example, what time zone will people work in and how will that affect the work of the group? How does the culture a group member is living in affect the way in which he or she views group work and collaboration to begin with? These are important issues that the group needs to explore as they undertake their work together.

Career Development and Transition of Team Members

Duarte and Snyder (2001) note, "When virtual team members are asked about the negative aspects of working in virtual teams, they almost always say that they are afraid that their careers will suffer. Their fear is that no one will keep track of their contributions and professional growth" (p. 81). Although career development is not of the utmost concern to the online learner, how the individual learner's contributions will be recognized in light of virtual team activity is of great concern. One way in which students can benefit from the application of collaborative work in an online class to potential career development is through the use of portfolios in which the products of collaborative work can be placed. Chapter Four is devoted to the important topic of evaluating and assessing individual student performance within collaborative group activity as well as looking at the performance of the group as a whole, including a more extensive discussion of the use of portfolios. Another topic involves transition of team members if students either add or drop the class while collaborative work is in process. Instructors will have to prepare the team in advance for this possibility as well as devise strategies for addressing it as it occurs.

Building Trust

Creating an atmosphere of safety and trust is critical to the development of a good working group online. One learner in an online class stated it beautifully when reflecting on the collaborative activity of the group: "This group seems to share an openness and supportiveness to ideas and exploration and that creates a safe environment in which to wonder, offer ideas, and participate in further exploration. It makes collaboration easier and more inviting and therefore more likely to happen. Clearly the environment/container created is an important factor for supporting and enriching collaborative efforts." *Judah*

Networking

Duarte and Snyder (2001) note that when virtual teams are formed in the work environment, the first few weeks of activity are often spent with just getting to know one another, establishing links, and networking. Instructors often wrongfully assume that an online class will not need this same type of activity and plunge students into collaborative work without giving them the time to get to know one another. Given the importance of safety and trust for collaboration to happen, it is critical that time for community formation be built into the design of the class before any collaborative group work is attempted. The likelihood for success increases with opportunities to get to know one another as people.

Developing and Adapting Team Practices

Online instructors often seek out what are considered to be best practices in online teaching to guide their own practice. This exploration becomes even more important when collaborative activity is included in an online course. Consulting with other online instructors and reading about successful frameworks for conducting collaborative work can keep an instructor from making the same mistakes that others have made and can help them build on successes. Clearly, an instructor wants the freedom to adapt the activity to meet the needs of his or her particular course or group. But having some frameworks to build from can reduce the amount of time that a group may struggle to get started and can promote the likelihood of a successful outcome for the activity.

VIRTUAL TEAM DYNAMICS

Other than our contribution to the literature on group dynamics in the online classroom (Palloff and Pratt, 2001), little to no literature has emerged looking at the dynamics of virtual teams. Once again, most of the attention to this important detail has occurred in the business world, where the effectiveness of a virtual team is a critical factor to the success of business projects. Instructors, however, can learn some valuable lessons from looking at virtual team dynamics in the business world and applying those lessons to the online academic setting.

Building Trust

Duarte and Snyder (2001) discuss the importance of building trust in virtual teams in order for the work of the team even to begin. They note three factors in building trust in the virtual environment.

Performance and Competence

These qualities include the ability to achieve results, follow through, and obtain resources. This attribute is focused on the leader of the team. However, in an academic setting, it would fall to the instructor. Does the instructor have the ability to form teams to achieve results? Does the instructor follow through by monitoring the working of the team, nudging team members when appropriate to make sure that the desired results are achieved? And finally, can the instructor point the team in the direction of appropriate resources to support them in completing their collaborative assignments?

Integrity

Duarte and Snyder describe integrity as "the alignment of actions and stated values" (p. 141), a critical factor in building trust in teams. The element of integrity applies not only to the instructor in an online course but also to all team members. Are all team members acting in a manner that is consistent with what they have agreed to in the team charter and what they say they will do? Are all team members carrying their weight in terms of completing assignments? Good communication between the instructor and all team members is the critical factor for ensuring that integrity exists; communication provides a means by which all team members feel included and valued in the collaborative process.

Concern for the Well-Being of Others

This characteristic includes an understanding of the impact of the team's work and actions on the people within the team. It is really a measure of the cohesiveness of the team and an awareness of how the work of one team affects the work of the class as a whole and vice versa. Including assessment of team cohesiveness and reflections on how well team members are working with and relating to one another can assist in developing this sense of concern for one another's well-being. In the final chapter, we include some examples of brief questionnaires and reflective tools that can assist the group in assessing its level of cohesiveness and the effectiveness of its teamwork.

Stages of Team Development

Another important aspect of virtual team dynamics is how the team develops and the stages the team moves through in this process. In a previous book, *Lessons from the Cyberspace Classroom* (2001), we discussed several models for looking at group or team development (McClure, 1998; McGrath and Hollingshead, 1994; Schopler, Abell, and Galinsky, 1998; and Tuckman and Jensen, 1977). What is common to most frameworks for team or group development is that they include a normative stage, in which group members are getting to know one another and are deciding how they will work together. This then leads to a stage of apparent unity or problem solving where the group begins to come together to do its work. However, as the group continues to move forward in its tasks, it is almost inevitable that some disagreement or conflict about process or tasks will emerge. This is critical to the development of the group. It is important that group members disagree as they move through their tasks—the development of a "groupthink" mentality, where everyone agrees in order to avoid conflict, often results in many members being dissatisfied with the results. Once the group is able to resolve its conflicts, it then moves into an action phase characterized by group harmony, during which the group is most productive. Finally, as the group ends its work, there is a termination phase. This may be followed by a regrouping if there are further tasks for the group to complete farther into the course or if group membership is shuffled by the instructor; in that case, a renewal of the process occurs.

Clearly, this developmental process needs to be considered when designing courses that include collaborative activity. The time factor for allowing groups to move through phases needs to be part of good course design. So, for example, if an instructor only allows one week for the development of an online team and the completion of its collaborative work, the likely outcome may be completion of the assignment, but it will be accompanied by frustration on the part of team members because they were not able to complete the group's developmental tasks that inevitably accompany the process.

In *Lessons from the Cyberspace Classroom,* we created and included a model depicting the elements of effective online groups. We present that model here in Figure 1.3, and include some additional discussion reflecting more recent lessons learned in the design and delivery of collaborative activity.

Notice the combined elements in the center of the model:

- Solve Problems
- Manage Conflict
- Develop Norms
- Process Information Together
- Communicate with One Another
- Connect

We see once again the elements of an online learning community presented earlier in this chapter: interaction and communication; a social constructivist context; presence; reflection and transformative learning; and the use of technology. We can conclude that in order to do effective group work and to develop effective groups online, a sense of community must be present. Without community, collaboration cannot occur, and collaboration and work in virtual teams assists in solidifying community. With this foundation, the stage is set for socially constructed meaning-making and acquisition of knowledge.

Based on this extensive argument for the importance of collaboration in an online class, we now turn our attention to the how's of collaboration—how do we, as

Figure 1.3. The Elements of Effective Online Groups.

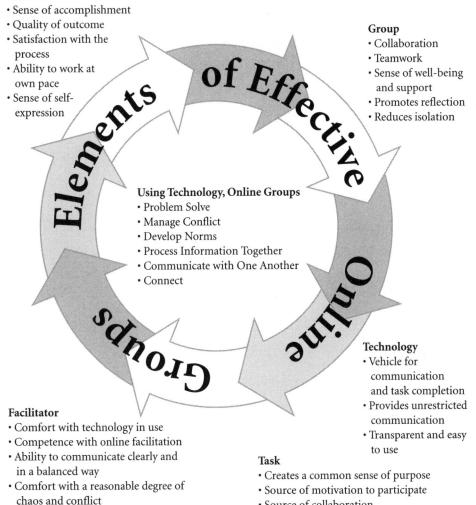

Individual
- Sense of accomplishment
- Quality of outcome
- Satisfaction with the process
- Ability to work at own pace
- Sense of self-expression

Group
- Collaboration
- Teamwork
- Sense of well-being and support
- Promotes reflection
- Reduces isolation

Using Technology, Online Groups
- Problem Solve
- Manage Conflict
- Develop Norms
- Process Information Together
- Communicate with One Another
- Connect

Technology
- Vehicle for communication and task completion
- Provides unrestricted communication
- Transparent and easy to use

Facilitator
- Comfort with technology in use
- Competence with online facilitation
- Ability to communicate clearly and in a balanced way
- Comfort with a reasonable degree of chaos and conflict
- Creates a safe container for the group
- Nurtures the development of relationships
- Promotes self-organization and empowerment

Task
- Creates a common sense of purpose
- Source of motivation to participate
- Source of collaboration

instructors, make it work? In the next chapter, we lay out the process for achieving successful online collaboration and provide tools for the instructor to assist a group in moving through that process to successful achievement of learning objectives.

SUMMARY POINTS TO REMEMBER ON COLLABORATION BASICS

- Successful collaboration depends on the creation of a learning community. Consequently, attention needs to be paid to community-building from the start of an online course.

- Collaboration addresses multiple learning styles and issues of culture.

- Collaboration serves to reduce the isolation that can occur online.

- Virtual teamwork not only allows students to gain competence in working in groups online, it also provides them an opportunity to test out real-world practices they are likely to face in the work world.

- Online groups move through phases, including a normative phase, a problem-solving phase, disagreement or conflict, an action phase, and termination.

- A strong sense of community can assist groups in moving through the phases of their development more effectively.

The Process of Online Collaboration

All too often, when collaborative activity is included in an online course, the approach is simply to write the activity into the syllabus, form dyads or teams, and assume that the students will be able to take it from there. In our experience, however, this approach often leads to frustration and resistance on the part of the students. At the very least, an explanation of the importance of and reasons for including collaborative activity in an online course can help reduce resistance going into the activity and can contribute to the success of the activity. The following are the stages of collaborative activity as we see them, along with some suggestions for instructor involvement at each stage and ways to make collaborative activity work.

THE STAGES OF COLLABORATION

Collaboration does not just happen. It takes planning and coordination on the part of the instructor to carry out collaborative activity successfully in an online class. Once the activity has begun, the instructor needs to stay present and involved in order to assure that students will engage with one another in a meaningful way. Collaborative activity requires that instructors empower students to take charge of the learning process. Consequently, it is important, before incorporating collaborative learning into an online course, that an instructor do a self-assessment to determine just how comfortable he or she is with letting go of control. Self-assessment questions for reflection include the following:

- How much do I know about small-group dynamics? Do I know enough to be able to intervene in a group if the process is not going well?
- How will I need to shift or change my teaching style to enable collaboration to happen?
- How comfortable do I feel letting go of control and allowing learners to take charge of the process?

The responses to these questions can determine whether collaborative activity will succeed or fail in an online course. The instructor must act as a facilitator or guide, allowing students to create their own learning process as they move through the phases of collaborative activity. It is the outcome of that process that is most critical; how the students get there should be of minimal interest to the instructor.

The following are the phases of instructor involvement in collaboration, along with some tips for successfully navigating each phase.

Set the Stage

Setting the stage involves a number of activities including providing an explanation of the importance of the collaborative work as well as clear guidelines for completing it. The results of case study research by Ge, Yamashiro, and Lee (2000) noted that student preparation prior to the engagement in collaborative activity significantly increases the cognitive achievement of participants. Preparation includes presenting an agenda and instructions for the activity as well as ensuring that students are comfortable with the technology in use. If students are clear about the nature of the activity and how they are to complete it, they are much more likely to pick up the gauntlet and move forward with minimal instructor intervention. The following reflection from a student after completing a collaborative activity illustrates the importance of setting the stage:

> How did we do it and why were we so successful?
>
> I think your expectations were clear, yet you left it up to us to figure out how to get the job done. Aside from producing the papers themselves, a key part of the assignment was to self-organize. Knowing that this was expected caused us to roll up our sleeves and pitch in from the very beginning. To me, this was probably the most important key to our success. In "real life," so many managers express frustration over the fact that their people don't self-manage, yet they fail to clearly express in the first place that this is expected. The fact that you assigned end results rather than "micro-managing" the process was also key; it is a style that too few are familiar with or comfortable adopting. *Julie*

Create the Environment

In order for collaborative activity to happen well, students need to have a place to meet and know the parameters of how they should connect. In other words, does all activity have to occur on the discussion board? If so, will there be a space created for each group to meet privately? Are phone calls and synchronous chat sessions permissible means for working together? Are face-to-face meetings allowed? Will the instructor be a part of the small group somehow, either through observation or direct participation in activities such as synchronous chats?

All of these questions need to be addressed in preparing students for an activity to assist them in knowing where to go to complete their work and what the "rules of engagement" might be. Julie adds to our understanding of this concept through her continued reflection on her experience.

> A logical framework was established early on in both assignments. The division of labor made sense and was fair, while creating opportunity for each of us to contribute in our own unique ways. Our individual commitments were strengthened by the fact that we all had a chance to weigh in on designing the process and to choose our respective roles. While there are some downsides to working asynchronisticly (sp?) and

primarily in writing, it does offer a level of built-in accountability by having everything there in front of everyone, in "black and white."

Model the Process

The instructor cannot simply set up a collaborative activity and walk away from it, leaving the learners to fend for themselves. Brookfield (1995) notes, "Students will be highly skeptical of group discussion if the teacher has not earned the right to ask students to work this way by first modeling her own commitment to the process" (p. 5). We believe that this is true for any form of collaborative activity. By modeling collaborative behavior in the course and by allowing students to negotiate some of the parameters within which they will work with one another and with the instructor, the instructor demonstrates what good collaboration looks like. As another student reflects:

> Last term I was more afraid of how I might be perceived when I posted my ideas on a topic or made a suggestion for action (in terms of organizing). I'm more comfortable now expressing my experiences and my ideas as well as suggestions for action and self-organizing. I've learned from watching others, reflecting upon other ideas, and that in turn brings out more of me. This group seems to share an openness and supportiveness to ideas and exploration and that creates a safe environment in which to wonder, offer ideas, and participate in further exploration. It makes collaboration easier and more inviting and therefore more likely to happen. Clearly the environment/container created [by the instructor] is an important factor for supporting and enriching collaborative efforts. *Judah*

Guide the Process

Modeling the process is a first step, but the instructor's responsibility does not end there. The instructor also has a responsibility to guide the process once it begins. Brookfield (1995) comments on this notion when he says, "A teacher cannot be a fly on the wall if that means being an unobtrusive observer. If you say nothing, this will be interpreted either as withholding of approval or as tacit agreement. Students will always be wondering what your opinion is about what they're doing. Better to give some brief indication of what's on your mind than to have students obsessed with whether your silence means disappointment or satisfaction with their efforts" (p. 11).

When it comes to collaborative activity, letting students know in advance how the instructor intends to be involved with the process and how he or she plans to guide it gives them the sense of confidence they need to move forward. The following note of appreciation at the close of a class indicates the importance of instructor facilitation in meeting learning objectives. It is shared to indicate the results that can occur when an instructor's guidance and modeling are successful.

> Last but not least, Rena, our facilitator, coach, confidant, and instructor, you modeled for us. I can only imagine with your busy schedule and traveling what it must be like, but you always kept your sense of humor, you were kind and sympathetic about our problems, and led us with compassion. Your comments and participation with the class were always inspiring, very supportive, and made us reflect on what was going on, or what was said. It was a great class. Thank you. *Gabe*

Evaluate the Process

The reflections from students that we have shared in the preceding sections of this list are snippets of evaluations of collaborative activities. It is important to include some form of evaluation at the close of any collaborative event or activity in an online class. This process allows the instructor to gain insight into whether the learning objectives of the specific activity were met and gives students the opportunity to debrief the experience. The final chapter has a more extensive discussion of how evaluation of collaborative activity can occur. At this point in our discussion, we want to emphasize two concepts regarding evaluation. First, student perceptions of the value of the collaborative activity they have experienced are critically important in determining the activity's success or failure, and second, the emphasis in evaluation should be on the learning generated by the activity. Brookfield and Preskill (1999) comment that student self-reporting as a means of evaluating an activity is inherently flawed. However, they state, "When students regularly document their perceptions of the contributions they are making to the ongoing exchange of ideas, they can learn an enormous amount about the conditions and behaviors that make discussion successful" (p. 217). We believe that the same is true in terms of evaluating collaborative activity, and we strongly encourage the inclusion of student self-assessment as a critical component of performance in an online course containing collaborative activity.

TOOLS FOR COLLABORATION

Effective movement through the stages of collaboration can be assisted through the use of tools and techniques that support the development of collaboration. Many of these tools specifically support setting the stage and creating the environment within which collaboration can happen. However, the tools can also serve as part of the modeling process for collaboration. We have often discussed, for example, the importance of establishing guidelines for an online course. However, when a collaborative activity occurs within that course, a different and specific set of guidelines needs to be presented to students in order to set the stage successfully. Repetition and redundancy can ensure that students accept and assimilate the expectations for collaboration and interact with one another more effectively. In this section, we review four such tools for collaboration: explanations for teams, guidelines and expectations, agreements, and buy-in, with some specific suggestions instructors can use to implement these tools in an online course.

Explanations for Teams

We cannot assume, as instructors, that our students will simply understand why collaboration is important. Often, students express resistance to participating in collaborative exercises due to past negative experiences wherein other students did not share the load, it was difficult to connect with one another across time zones, or because of the amount of work collaborative activity entails. Consequently, in setting the stage for collaborative work, the instructor can ease the degree of resistance in the group by simply explaining why the activity is occurring and how it contributes to learning objectives for the course. The following is an example of such an explanation to students. Our thanks to our colleague Cheryl Doran for contributing this example.

> In this course, you will work individually as well as in teams of two. The intent of teamwork is to encourage dialogue and debate so that you will discuss issues in greater depth than postings to the CourseRoom allow. Learning can be enhanced when collaboratively constructing knowledge.

During the scope of this quarter, each dyad will engage in the development of an ongoing project—a simulated strategic-quality planning activity. The project is broken down into segments that are assigned on a unit-by-unit basis, building logically toward the final product.

The instructor will be developing dyads based in part on common interests and experiences. For that reason, it is particularly important that you post your personal profile as early in the week as possible. Feel free to contact each other once your information has been posted. When working in dyads, it is helpful to establish ground rules and expectations at the very beginning of the quarter. Here are a few points you may wish to discuss as you organize your working relationship.

1. Modes of communication.

2. Sharing of responsibilities.

3. Accountability. Think about what you value in terms of team participation. How will each of you be accountable? Promptness of response, notification of when a delay is inevitable, quality of contribution, and whether a team member participated in each team assignment might be some issues to consider. How will you assess your own participation?

Your instructor is available and very willing to help with your dyad process. Please ask for assistance, feedback, or support as needed.

Guidelines and Expectations

We have already discussed the importance of creating guidelines for student participation in collaborative activity. The guidelines help both to set the stage for students and to create the container within which the collaborative activity will occur. The following suggestions for instructors, contributed by one of our learners who teaches online (Dell, 2004), can assist instructors in developing collaborative learning activities and help learners to work effectively in activities that involve online collaboration. Attention to all of these issues should help to ensure success in collaborative work. Dell's suggestions have been drawn from the work of Johnson and Johnson (2000), Kagan (1994), Palloff and Pratt (2003), Millis (n.d.), Bailey and Luetkehans (1998), and Ko and Rossen (2001), as well as from her own experience.

- Explain the importance of collaborative group work and make it a require-ment of the course—not an option. Although some learners tend to prefer to work alone, allowing them to do so reduces the likelihood of a mean-ingful learning experience.

- Form groups that are heterogeneous with respect to gender, age, ethnicity, learning styles, abilities, and experiences. Groups of two to four learners are best. Instructors and designers should consider the purpose of the group and the cooperative structures that will be used as they determine the number of teams.

- Allow time for ice-breaking and team-building activities, which allow learn-ers to begin to form a sense of community. The activity may be a specific team-building structure or it may simply encourage students to introduce themselves to one another.

- Give clear instructions and guidelines regarding not only the assignments, but also the method and tools of communication that will be used. Start simple to give students time to understand the structures and methods of communication.

- Set reasonable goals and provide a place for the group to interact. Many course management systems provide areas intended solely for this pur-pose. The tools available, such as asynchronous group discussion boards, live chat, and interactive white boards vary with the course management system chosen.

- Supervise the group's progress and be available to prompt or assist groups that are having difficulty. Your "presence" will help to ensure participation by all members. Be prepared to intervene and mediate conflicts of an inter-personal nature without taking sides. Suggest that the group explore alter-natives and reach consensus.

- Design evaluation criteria to include peer evaluation. This rewards extraor-dinary team members while at the same time appropriately evaluates non-contributing members.

- Provide a place for the team to share their work and learning products with the larger learning community. Many projects can be posted on a Web site or added as an attachment to a discussion thread.

Agreements

The use of "team charters" or agreements has been noted to be of significant importance in promoting learner satisfaction with collaborative learning experiences online (Doran, 2001). A team charter serves as an agreement or contract among members, outlining how they will interact together, determining the roles each member will play in the collaborative activity, and creating benchmarks and deadlines for the completion and submission of collaborative work.

Generally speaking, it is a good idea to assign the completion of a team charter early in a course where collaborative group work will be used, or at least as soon as groups are formed, so that it can serve to guide the activities of the group. A requirement of the charter activity should be posting the charter online so that team members can refer back to it, edit it as necessary, or amend it as conditions change. Providing sample team charters assists the group in understanding the concept and in the development of their own charter. The following are a few simple guidelines for the creation of team charters that work well to get students started:

In order to make group work successful, all group members must agree to abide by norms established by the group. As your group is forming, please reach consensus on the following items and post your group's charter to the main discussion board:

- *How will your group identify itself?* Your group may choose a name under which to function.

- *How will the group communicate?* For example, through the discussion board, e-mail, virtual classroom, phone, or a combination of methods?

- *What day during the week will the discussion begin?*

- *How quickly should group members be expected to respond to e-mails or discussion board postings?* For example, within twelve hours, within one day, and so on.

- *What role or duties will each person in the group perform?* Possible roles include initiator, secretary, liaison to the instructor, motivator, organizer, and so forth.

- *Who is responsible for posting group responses to the main discussion board?*

- *How will the group handle a member who is not participating?*
- *Discuss any other topics that are unique to your group.*

The following is an example of how the development of a team charter might be included in the syllabus of an online course:

We will work together to jointly develop a Team Charter for the course. A charter will clarify our purpose, identify our deliverables, define our responsibilities (operating guidelines), and bring us together as a team. It will also help us monitor our results and evaluate our progress. (We will revisit it in Weeks Four, Eight, and Twelve.) We will build the charter around three headings: purpose, deliverables, and operating guidelines. The statement of purpose is a single sentence outlining why we are here. The statement of deliverables is a bulleted list (five to seven items) describing the results we want to achieve. Operating guidelines define how we will work together and how we will treat one another; it will be in the form of a bulleted list of five to seven items, each starting with the word "we." Use the following headings to develop your posting. Keep the process simple. It should take you no longer than a half-hour to do this. Also, while working on this, designate one person or two people to pull the charter together to be circulated to and approved by the rest of us. Someone may choose to volunteer for this role or you may negotiate it among you. If nobody steps forward, I'll be forced to "volunteer" someone in the group, but I suspect that will be unlikely!

Here are the headings:

- Our purpose is to (answer in one sentence)
- Our deliverables include: (answer in five to seven clear, concise bulleted statements)
- Operating Guidelines: (answer in five to seven clear, concise bulleted statements beginning with the word "we." For example, We complete postings on time.)

Your posting is due Friday at midnight Pacific time. I will create a folder labeled Team Charter for this purpose.

Buy-in

The team charter process helps to ensure buy-in from all members of the team. Through the negotiation process with one another, the group members form a contract for their learning. Should a team member not fulfill that agreement, it then becomes the responsibility of the instructor to follow up with that learner and remind him or her of the agreed-upon responsibilities and tasks.

When a team charter is not used, it is still possible to use other means by which to get learner buy-in. The syllabus should be constructed with enough detail and description of collaborative activities so as to serve as the foundation for how that activity will occur. Asking learners to signal their agreement to the syllabus at the beginning of the course can also serve as a contract between instructor and learner and among learners. In addition, individual learning contracts can engage learners in a negotiation process with the instructor by which they agree to fulfill all responsibilities of collaboration as a part of their overall learning for the course.

Regardless of how it is accomplished, a contract for collaborative activity should be established so that if a student begins to neglect his or her responsibilities to the team, the instructor can intervene and remind that student of the agreements made at the beginning of the course.

Although the use of the collaborative tools just presented can help to ensure the successful outcome of collaborative activity, life does intervene and problems can and do occur. In the next chapter, we explore the issues and concerns that can interfere with successful outcomes of collaborative work and make suggestions for interventions.

SUMMARY POINTS TO REMEMBER ON THE PROCESS OF ONLINE COLLABORATION

- In order to achieve successful collaborative activity, attention needs to be paid to the four phases of activity: set the stage, model the process, guide the process, and evaluate the process.

- Before including collaborative activity in an online course, the instructor should conduct a critical self-reflection to determine how comfortable he or she truly is with this form of activity. An instructor who is less comfortable with empowering students to take control of their learning process is less likely to experience success in collaborative work.

- By utilizing tools such as explanations for teams and team charters, the instructor can effectively set the stage and model the process of collaboration online.

- Effective buy-in for collaborative activity can occur by using the tools to set the stage and can create a contract for collaborative activity.

- Do not assume that students will jump at the opportunity to collaborate. Instead, anticipate that they will be resistant and use measures to counter that resistance, such as explanations for teams, early on in the course.

Collaboration Challenges

I n the previous chapter we discussed how to maximize the process of collaboration; however, given that instructors and their students are human, there are always factors that can get in the way of successful outcomes. Some are elements that are beyond the control of the instructor, such as technical difficulties or institutional mandates. But others, such as dyads or teams that are not interacting well, are elements the instructor does have some power to deal with. In this chapter, we review some of the elements that can interfere with the successful outcome of collaborative activity and make suggestions for instructor interventions that may help turn the tide and promote a more positive result.

THINGS THAT GO BUMP IN THE NIGHT

As we have discussed, students do not necessarily enter collaborative activities willingly. They may have experienced collaborative activities in other courses that did not go well. They may not want to exert the effort that collaborative activity takes or expend the extra time demanded of them to coordinate with others to complete the task. Many students come into an online experience believing that such courses promote independent study and are resentful when asked to work with others.

Although focused on interagency collaboration rather than student collaboration, the Arizona PARTNERS Organization (Davis, 1997) has created a collaboration manual that lists some of the challenges to collaboration, which we have annotated with regard to online student groups:

- *Turf protection and mistrust:* Individuals may not be open to new ideas or to sharing the information or resources they find through their research.
- *Decision-making processes:* Groups need to determine how they will make decisions and hold to that process.
- *Limited resources:* In an online class, this relates to time limitations and limited access to information.
- *Dropping out:* Attrition is a problem in online group collaboration; shifts in membership as an activity is underway can cause significant problems.
- *Reduced participation:* Some members may participate more or contribute more than others, creating resentment and conflict among group members.
- *Broad representation:* Groups should include a cross section of the larger class.
- *Communication:* Groups working together collaboratively need to maintain open and regular communication so that all members feel included.
- *Solid leadership:* Groups that select a leader to guide their process are more likely to succeed in a collaborative task.
- *Time commitment:* Groups need to know up front how much time a collaborative activity will take and each member needs to commit to that time.

We add a few more items to this list based on our own experience and the experiences of our colleagues:

- *Teams that play too much:* Some teams or team members actually over-participate in collaborative activities, in effect creating a situation of expectations that are so high that they may not get met.
- *Courseware issues and limitations:* Some course management systems simply do not easily allow for collaborative work and can be a source of frustration.

- *Technical difficulties:* Difficulty with access to the course, computer viruses, and other technical crises can wreak havoc with collaborative assignments. Additional difficulties can occur as the result of lack of familiarity with software.

- *Course design issues:* Some courses are designed to mimic their on-the-ground counterparts, with collaborative activity simply an add-on.

- *Cultural differences:* Issues of culture may expose potential differences in communication style, how conflict is handled, and the like. Joo (1999) notes that cultural issues in online courses emerge in the areas of content, Web design and the use of media, writing styles and structures, and perceptions of the role of the student and instructor. To address these concerns, instructors should seek out, to whatever degree possible, materials that represent more than one cultural viewpoint. Instructors can also encourage students to bring materials to the course or to their group that represent the views of their culture or to share their cultural perspective so as to increase the awareness of all group members.

- *Faculty issues:* Some instructors create collaborative activities in their courses but have difficulty handing control over to the learners.

For the purpose of this discussion, these issues will be grouped into four larger categories: participation, leadership and decision making, course and activity design, and cultural issues. We will review each of these categories, with suggestions for dealing with the challenges.

PARTICIPATION CHALLENGES

It would be ideal if an instructor were simply able to form teams and let them loose to do their collaborative work, with assurance that all students would participate equally. Unfortunately, that is rarely the case. Depending on where the collaborative activity falls in a course schedule, students may be adding or dropping the class or responding to other demands, such as exams and papers due in other courses or family demands, that may interfere with their ability to participate well. The latest computer worm or virus may cause computer crashes that also hinder students' ability to participate. Differences in expectations or in willingness to collaborate may also interfere, or, conversely, overly high expectations for participation on the part of team members may cause problems.

Because of these issues, instructors should take some precautionary measures at the start of a course that involves collaborative work. The following suggestions may be helpful:

• *Set the stage for collaboration.* As we discussed in the previous chapter, pay particular attention to setting the stage for collaborative work through the development of team charters and by providing guidelines and expectations for collaborative work and participation. Ask students to buy into collaborative processes through the use of contracts or agreements about how they will work with one another and participate.

• *Don't encourage over- or under-participation.* Instructors need to monitor the activity of teams and should intervene if it looks as though participation in a dyad or team is uneven. Overachievers should be slowed down and underachievers encouraged to get into the game. A simple e-mail or phone conversation will often help with participation concerns.

• *Address technical difficulties swiftly.* There is nothing more damaging to collaborative work than a student's inability to access the course or contact his or her teammates. Because it is so critical for students to stay engaged with the activity, alternatives to working from home if technical problems occur should be suggested up front, such as working from a computer lab, the library, a workplace, or a friend's house.

• *Provide instruction and information about conflict management and conflict resolution.* McGrath and Hollingshead (1994) note that in online groups, the ability to resolve conflict is one of the central tasks to be accomplished in order for goals to be achieved and tasks completed. Conflict is more likely to surface in collaborative activity. Consequently, the instructor should be prepared for it and should prepare students for dealing with it. Often, we let our learners know that we would like them to try to resolve the conflict between them first, but if that is not possible, we ask the group leader to signal us that our intervention is needed. If the group leader is the problem, then other members of the group know they are free to come to us with their concerns. Reflections on conflict management should be included in assessment of collaborative activity, as this creates another forum for students to learn about the important task of managing conflict online.

• *Maximize participation through group composition* (Ragoonaden and Bordeleau, 2000). Issues such as personal, professional, and cultural backgrounds can be a help or a hindrance to a collaborative process depending on the individual members of the group. To minimize group difficulties, negotiations between team members should occur at the start of any activity so that members know how each expects to participate, any limitations on participation that may occur, preferred styles of communication, conflicting demands, and so forth.

CHALLENGES IN LEADERSHIP AND DECISION MAKING

Closely related to the issue of conflict and conflict management are the issues of leadership and decision making. Research has shown that the more clearly students are prepared for collaborative work, including understanding how roles are defined in a collaborative learning situation, the more likely they will feel satisfied with the experience and the outcome (Borden and Perkins, 1999; Davis, 1997; Ge, Yamashiro, and Lee, 2000). Furthermore, students must decide on a decision-making strategy at the start so as to minimize the possibility of conflict. Will decisions be made by consensus? Will the majority rule? These are questions that students need to ask and answer in order to negotiate a collaborative process that contains a final collaborative product. The following student quotations describe the impact of a smooth leadership and decision-making process related to their satisfaction with the outcome:

> In reading back through the beginning posts from each, it seems all it takes is a beginning idea/suggestion to get the ball rolling. Then another person responds and often adds another idea/refinement/ further development (or a question). And as a group, we are able to build on the momentum until we are self-organized enough to begin the work on content. And then we work on content and when the next organizing need comes up, someone calls it out or asks a question and someone else responds with an idea or an action and we're off again. So someone who has an idea expresses it, others willingly hear it, take it in, build upon it, and/or ask clarifying question(s), and others support the ideas generated. We're not second-guessing each other—more an experience of going with and adding to the flow. *Judah*

> I think we all came in with a solid understanding of the concept of shared leadership. None of us spent any time trying to figure out who

was "in charge," jockeying for position, status, or control. And we didn't waste any time waiting for someone to tell us what to do. *Julie*

When leadership and decision making go well, collaborative processes go well.

COURSE AND ACTIVITY DESIGN CHALLENGES

Ragoonaden and Bordeleau (2000) note that the regular inclusion of collaborative activities in an online course is critical to the development of an ongoing collaborative process. They further note that when a course is designed using what would be considered traditional teaching methods, such as lecture and discussion, and where assignments are predominantly independent research assignments, the addition of some collaborative activities can be considered burdensome to students. Courses designed with collaboration in mind should use collaborative processes throughout. These activities should not be considered secondary to the production of other individual assignments, but in order to create alignment in the course, should be considered the primary means by which assignments are completed.

The model of collaboration we presented in Figure 1.2 in Chapter One shows that the social constructivist context of an online course should be the guiding factor in course design. The goal is to reduce isolation and maximize learning potential by creating social presence. Consequently, promoting independent work in an online course runs counter to the overarching objective—the creation of a sense of community through collaboration and support of collaborative activity through the vehicle of the learning community. Collaboration, then, should be a theme that runs throughout the course.

In order to design and deliver collaborative courses successfully, instructors need to assess themselves to determine their comfort level with this form of activity. Ragoonaden and Bordeleau (2000) noted that although the instructor was present and available in the courses they studied, his focus was predominantly on answering questions and providing feedback on academic work. The more students relied on the instructor to play this role, the less they relied on one another for it. The instructor needs to feel comfortable truly turning over the reigns to the learners in the learning process in order for collaboration to be successful. We often ask instructors in our presentations, "How comfortable do you feel, as an instructor, with the inclusion of collaborative learning assignments, personal interaction, the concept of promoting knowledge in learners, and giving control of the learning process to the learners?" The answers to these questions may make or break collaborative work.

One last factor to consider in the area of course and activity design challenges is the course management system. Although many of the popular course management systems allow for the creation of private spaces in which small groups can work, some still do not. This does not mean that collaborative activity can only work where small-group spaces can be created, but it certainly helps. Creativity is the key when the technology does not adequately support collaborative activity. Groups and dyads can be encouraged to work via e-mail, instant-messaging programs, or if all else fails, by phone. Although not ideal, these forms of technology do work in getting the collaborative job done. Finally, as with any form of online activity, students must feel comfortable with the technology being used. If a means of communicating other than online is to be used for collaborative work, the instructor needs to be sure that students know how to use it to avoid technical challenges and frustrations that might interfere with their success.

THE CHALLENGE OF CULTURAL DIFFERENCES

DuPraw and Axner (1997) list six fundamental patterns of cultural difference:

- *Different communication styles.* These include language usage and the importance of nonverbal communication. The online environment may enhance or detract from some of the cultural elements of communication style.

- *Different attitudes toward conflict.* Some cultures avoid conflict while others welcome it. DuPraw and Axner note that written communication might be a favored means to resolve conflict when cultural differences are present. Consequently, the online environment may actually be a benefit when conflict emerges in a culturally diverse group, allowing them to work through that conflict in writing.

- *Different approaches to completing tasks.* Some of the differences emerge from the degree of importance that is placed on relationship building for the completion of collaborative work. Another issue is differing access to resources and differing notions about time and timeliness.

- *Different decision-making styles.* Individuals' attitudes about their own roles in decision making may vary by culture. Some cultures value democratic decision making, while others defer to the will of the leader.

- *Different attitudes toward disclosure.* In some cultures people feel uncomfortable about displaying emotions, dealing with conflict, or sharing personal information with a group.

- *Different approaches to knowing.* In some cultures people prefer finding information through researching literature while in others, people prefer to learn through experience or by talking to people who have experienced the same challenges they are facing. In other words, some cultural styles employ a more cognitive way of knowing while others use a more community-based way of knowing.

What is important here is to understand the cultural differences involved in approaching a collaborative task and to account for them in the process. Incorporating cultural differences into a collaborative process does not need to be a challenge; instead, it can be an enhancement to the outcome of collaborative work. DuPraw and Axner suggest that being open to learning from other cultures, respecting the differences, listening to one another, and being aware of power imbalances can help people overcome the challenges of working cross-culturally. Ragoonaden and Bordeleau (2000) note that students can come to appreciate and look forward to cross-cultural exchanges in online work and that these exchanges support the development of community online. Cross-cultural groups add a richness to collaborative work that cannot be engineered, only appreciated.

FINAL THOUGHTS ON CHALLENGES TO COLLABORATION ONLINE

Ragoonaden and Bordeleau (2000) looked at some of the factors we have been discussing regarding elements that may interfere with successful collaborative activity. Their study yielded the following recommendations for including collaborative activity in an online course:

- Collaborative tasks should be an integral element of the course design and should be offered at regular intervals. As much as possible, collaborative tasks have to be evaluated on an equal par with individual work.

- Distance learners should be encouraged to construct learning together through meaningful collaborative tasks that allow for pertinent interaction. These collaborative tasks must be based on a constructivist approach rather than a transmission-type approach.

- Group composition has to be undertaken with great care by attempting to match personal, professional, cultural, and academic backgrounds. (Conclusion, ¶ 4)

The bottom line is that good planning and preparation for collaborative work can head off or resolve many of the woes that may befall a collaborative activity before they even occur. The following student reflection demonstrates just how effective this can be:

> I learned to respect the power of online group work during this course. I was truly amazed by the way our groups organized for the group assignments.
> I learned that it is OK to let others take the lead and to do what you can—even if that's not what you are used to doing.
> I learned the importance of communicating (openly and honestly) what is going on in your life so others can support you.
> I learned that others will support you—even when they've never met you. *Kim*

SUMMARY POINTS TO REMEMBER ON COLLABORATION CHALLENGES

- Collaborative courses should involve collaboration throughout the process.
- Effective planning is the key to avoiding collaboration challenges.
- For collaboration to be successful, the instructor needs to do a self-assessment to ensure that he or she is truly comfortable with this form of activity and does not view it as an "add on" to more important work.
- The instructor should provide the learners with technical training and ensure that adequate technical support is available so that technical difficulties do not interfere with successful collaboration.

- The instructor should encourage students to choose a leader who will assign roles to enable the process to flow smoothly.

- The instructor needs to intervene in cases of over- and under-participation to minimize frustration and conflict.

- Students should be encouraged to celebrate difference and diversity in their groups and appreciate the richness that a diverse learning experience brings.

Assessment and Evaluation of Collaborative Work

Evaluation of students in an online course can be challenging. Explaining to students how they were evaluated can be even more challenging. In order to assess student performance in collaborative activity effectively, the instructor needs to understand basic principles of student assessment. Angelo and Cross (1993) believe that in order for assessment to be effective, it must be embedded in and aligned with the design of the course. They note a number of characteristics of effective classroom assessment: it is learner-centered, teacher-directed, mutually beneficial, formative, context-specific, ongoing, and firmly rooted in good practice. Although they are discussing assessment techniques for the face-to-face classroom, these same principles can be applied effectively to the online classroom.

As we have noted in previous work (Palloff and Pratt, 2003), the following principles should guide student assessment in an online course:

- Design learner-centered assessments that include self-reflection.

- Design and include grading rubrics to assess contributions to the discussion as for assignments, projects, and the collaboration itself.

- Include collaborative assessments through publicly posting papers along with comments from student to student.

- Encourage students to develop skills in providing feedback by providing guidelines to good feedback and by modeling what is expected.

- Use assessment techniques that fit the context and align with learning objectives.

- Design assessments that are clear, easy to understand, and likely to work in the online environment.

- Ask for and incorporate student input into how assessment should be conducted (pp. 101–102).

When working collaboratively, all of these principles become critically important. Students need a road map not only to guide the activity, but also to know how that activity will be assessed and evaluated. Morgan and O'Reilly (1999) offer six key qualities for assessment of online students: a clear rationale and consistent pedagogical approach; explicit values, aims, criteria, and standards; authentic and holistic tasks; a facilitative degree of structure; sufficient and timely formative assessment; and awareness of the learning context and perceptions. According to Morgan and O'Reilly, the assessments and assessment criteria should not only be clear and easy to understand, they should also align with the instructional approaches used in the course, the context in which the course occurs, and the competencies to be assessed. In addition, assessments should be formative—meaning that they occur throughout the course and inform practice—and summative— meaning that they occur at the end of the course and assess cumulative learning from the course. We will now review each of the guiding principles for student assessment in relationship to collaborative work online.

LEARNER-CENTERED ASSESSMENT, INCLUDING SELF-ASSESSMENT

Given that a well-designed online course should be focused and centered on the learner, it follows that student evaluation within that course should be the same. The reflective process that should be included in an online course provides the basis for learner-centered assessment. Students should be given credit for self-reflection and the activity should be incorporated into the design and expectations for the online course. Each collaborative activity should contain a reflective component. At the very least, students should be asked to reflect on their participation in the activity and their contributions to the group. In addition, asking students to reflect on the process not only allows them to evaluate the activity, but also gives the instructor important formative and summative information that can be incorporated into future iterations of the assignment. The following questions might be asked to assist students in doing this type of assessment:

- How comfortable did you feel as a member of this group?
- Do you feel that all group members' voices were heard and accepted?
- How did your group establish roles and leadership?
- What means did you use to communicate with one another? Were they successful, in your opinion?
- Did you feel comfortable with that process and feel that you had adequate input?
- How well did you work together as a team?
- Did you encounter any problems as you worked together? How did you overcome or resolve them?
- How did you feel about this assignment? Did it help you to understand the content of this course better? Why or why not?

Another form of learner-centered assessment that is useful in collaborative work is the creation of a portfolio. Although the products of collaborative activities are often team products, creating a portfolio that includes both the individual contributions of the student and the final product is a good way for the instructor to assess how much work the individual student did and give the student an opportunity to showcase his or her work in light of the larger project. The creation of a portfolio that includes both individual and collaborative projects can also serve as an incentive for participation if learners understand that they will be assessed as individuals as well as members of a team. In addition, a portfolio is useful for students as they move out of the academic arena in search of a job. The portfolio can be shown to prospective employers to demonstrate what the student is capable of producing on their own as well as when they are part of a team.

RUBRICS AND EXPECTATIONS

Conrad and Donaldson (2004) describe a rubric as a tool that "defines the performance levels for each gradable activity element" (p. 26). As such, rubrics provide students with a concrete way of evaluating their own performance as well as the performance of the members of their team. Having a well-developed rubric assists the instructor with the "How am I doing?" questions that often emerge in an online course. Both the instructor and the student can evaluate performance by using the rubric and then comparing results. If rubrics are linked to course expectations and students are directed to use them for assessment of themselves and their peers, students will end the course with a clear picture of their performance. This activity not only provides a realistic picture of how a student interacted with course material and their peers, it also reduces the possibilities of grade inflation, dissatisfaction, and grade appeals by providing evaluative material that is objective and quantifiable. Performance in collaborative work is frequently seen as hazy and difficult to measure. The use of a rubric for assessment of self and peers takes the guesswork out of this process.

Designing rubrics for collaborative work does not have to be complicated. The rubrics should include performance measures for both individual and group or team work. Exhibit 4.1 shows how rubrics might be constructed to accompany a course that involves collaborative work.

COLLABORATIVE ASSESSMENT

A simple rule to remember when assessing collaborative work is that collaborative activities are best assessed collaboratively. Although Angelo and Cross (1993) note that assessment should be instructor-directed, putting the responsibility for assessing collaborative activity wholly on the instructor's shoulders omits an important component of assessment, that of peer or team assessment. The instructor should certainly retain the determination about what to assess, how to assess it, and how to respond to any evaluation material gathered through the reflective material submitted by students. It is, after all, the instructor's responsibility to record a final grade for the course and to follow up with those who are not performing.

EXHIBIT 4.1. Sample Rubrics for Assessing Collaborative Work.

Group Presentations Rubric

Objectives	Low Performance	At or Below Average	At or Above Average	Exemplary Performance
Teamwork	**1 point** Only one person presented. Unclear team roles.	**2 points** Clear team roles but unequal contributions.	**3 points** Clear roles, equal contributions.	**4 points** Clear roles, balanced contributions, good transitions between presenters.
Presentation Style/Delivery	**1 point** No introduction or overview. Poor style (disorganized, difficult to follow). Went above or below page limits.	**2 points** Appropriate introduction to topic but opinions expressed inadequately or vaguely. Barely met page limits.	**3 points** Generally good delivery, presents arguments or opinions in a convincing manner.	**4 points** Excellent style, involving matching written and nonverbal styles (graphics). Creative and imaginative.
Information/ Content	**1 point** Does not have grasp of information, opinions stated but not supported by information. For second presentation: no discussion on search tools chosen to fulfill the task. Did not rank Web sites according to reliability.	**2 points** Incorporates few facts or little information to support ideas or opinions. For second presentation: search engines or other tools only cursorily mentioned. Gave a brief listing of rankings.	**3 points** Demonstrates grasp of knowledge. Incorporates ample hints or strategies. For second presentation: mentioned the specific search tools used and why. Gave a full listing of rankings.	**4 points** Complete and accurate presentation of important, related strategies or facts. Good use of technical or subject vocabulary. For second presentation: provided several reasons for using selected databases or search engines. Provided reasons for the ranking of topic Web sites.

Rubric for Individual Performance on a Team

	Needs Improvement: 1	Developing: 2	Accomplished: 3	Exemplary: 4
General Attitude	Often is publicly critical of the project or the work of other members of the group. Often has a negative attitude about the task(s).	Occasionally is publicly critical of the project or the work of other members of the group but most of the time has a positive attitude about the task(s).	Rarely is publicly critical of the project or the work of others. Often has a positive attitude about the task(s).	Never is publicly critical of the project or the work of others. Always has a positive attitude about the task(s).
Working with Others	Rarely listens to, shares with, or supports the efforts of others. Often is not a good team player.	Often listens to, shares with, and supports the efforts of others, but sometimes is not a good team member.	Usually listens to, shares with, and supports the efforts of others. Does not cause "waves" in the group.	Almost always listens to, shares with, and supports the efforts of others. Tries to keep people working well together.
Collaboration	Rarely provides useful ideas when participating in the group and in classroom discussion. May refuse to participate.	Sometimes provides useful ideas when participating in the group and in classroom discussion.	Usually provides useful ideas when participating in the group and in classroom discussion. A strong group member who tries hard.	Routinely provides useful ideas when participating in the group and in classroom discussion. A definite leader who contributes a lot of effort.

Preparedness	Often forgets needed materials or is rarely ready to get to work.	Almost always brings needed materials but sometimes needs to settle down and get to work.	Almost always brings needed materials to class and is ready to work.	Brings needed materials to class and is always ready to work.
Focus on Task and Time Management	Rarely focuses on the task and what needs to be done, and does not respect deadlines. Lets others do the work. Group has to adjust deadlines or work responsibilities because of this person's inadequate time management and lack of collaboration.	Focuses on the task and what needs to be done some of the time. Other group members must sometimes nag, prod, and remind to keep this person on task. Tends to procrastinate, but finally always gets things done by the deadlines.	Focuses on the task and what needs to be done most of the time and uses time well throughout the project. Other group members can count on this person. However, may have procrastinated on one thing or another.	Consistently stays focused on the task and what needs to be done. Very self-directed. Uses time well throughout the project to ensure things get done on time. Does not procrastinate.

However, the information gathered through collaborative assessment should not be given less emphasis than the information gathered through the instructor's direct observation or evaluation.

Students often have far more information about the workings of a small group than does the instructor. If encouraged and guided, students will share that information so that appropriate grading can occur. As mentioned in the previous chapter, however, instructors need to guard against possible scapegoating in grading, wherein students grade a peer far lower than deserved due to interpersonal difficulties in the group. Consequently, the instructor needs to retain "veto power" in grading. Information about assessment and evaluation should be built into the course guidelines and expectations communicated to students at the beginning of the course so as to prepare students for their responsibilities in providing constructive feedback and fair assessment of their peers.

Angelo and Cross (1993) state, "By cooperating in assessment, students reinforce their grasp of the course content and strengthen their own skills at self-assessment" (pp. 4–5). By collaboratively assessing student progress, students come to believe in the basic tenets of a learning community—they find themselves involved in something that is greater than the sum of its parts. Not only are they engaged in a learning process, they have the ability to improve that process for themselves and others through feedback to the instructor. In so doing, students increase their ability to reflect and provide good feedback. Providing guidelines for feedback can be a help to students as they take on this role.

GUIDELINES FOR FEEDBACK

In *The Virtual Student* (Palloff and Pratt, 2003) we noted the importance of prepping students for giving one another meaningful feedback on their work. When collaborative assignments are given, this becomes more critical, as students are often reticent to be honest about the participation or lack thereof of their peers. Conrad and Donaldson (2004) note, "In an engaged learning environment, peers often have the best perspective on whether their teammates are providing valuable contributions to the learning community. Therefore, learning environments that encourage collaborative activities should incorporate peer evaluations in the assessment process. . . . The key to effective peer feedback is that it be constructive and encourage improvement" (p. 27). Sharing the following guidelines for effective feedback with students and encouraging students to use them in the development and delivery of feedback can help to alleviate the problems and concerns involved with using student feedback as an evaluative tool:

- Don't just make up feedback as you go along. Plan ahead.

- Before you start to type, think first about what you want to say. Get your ideas straight in your head, and figure out how they all fit together.

- Make some notes before typing a message online. This helps you figure out what you need to say.

- Use short paragraphs. This forces you to express yourself with a minimum of words.

- When you write something, make sure that people will understand you. After you type in a message—and before you send it—try reading it out loud. Sometimes sentences that seem to be okay when you're typing don't really work when you read them back.

- Some people quote a huge message, then place a brief comment at the end, such as "I agree with this!" or "Me, too!" This can be annoying to the person who has to scroll all the way through the message, looking for the part that you wrote. It makes more sense for you to quote only a few important sentences that summarize the message adequately, and place your comment after that.

- Simply saying that you agree with something doesn't add much to the conversation. Why not tell people why you agree? You can state some of the reasons why you feel the way you do. This way, you will look like a person who thinks carefully about things and considers all the facts.

- You should always read what you have written before you send your message. Not only will this help you spot errors in spelling, phrasing, and grammar, but you may also notice that you don't sound as friendly as you would like. Make sure your message is worded professionally and not harshly to avoid insulting those who will read it or inadvertently "flaming" other members of the group. (pp. 171–172)

In addition, rubrics that include points for providing effective feedback are likely to encourage students to use the guidelines in constructing feedback and to be more honest and constructive in the feedback they deliver to one another. Students should be encouraged to maintain professional levels of communication with one another at all times and should not assume that the friendly relationships they have had in working with one another will cure all ills. We never know how our comments will be perceived online. Consequently, care needs to be taken in all written communication.

ASSESSMENT THAT ALIGNS WITH CONTEXT AND LEARNING OBJECTIVES

Morgan and O'Reilly (1999) note that if an online course is designed with clear guidelines and objectives, contain tasks and assignments that are relevant not only to the subject matter but to students' lives as well, and students understand what is expected of them, assessment will be in alignment with the course as a whole and will not be seen as a separate and cumbersome task. Keeping this principle in mind also promotes the use of assessments that move beyond tests and quizzes. Although tests and quizzes are useful in assessing some aspects of collaborative work, they should not be the main means of assessment. For example, in a mathematics class, the instructor may set up collaborative homework forums and group problem-solving activities, but may still use tests and quizzes to assess individual acquisition of skills. This grouping of assessment activities would be in alignment with course objectives, the subject matter being studied, and the need to determine competency or the acquisition of skills.

Many online instructors have noted the difficulty of using tests and quizzes as effective assessments of student learning. Many feel that more authentic assessments, such as projects, papers, and artifacts that integrate course concepts, are more effective means by which to assess student learning online. Therefore, self-reflections, peer assessments, and rubrics align more closely with the objectives of an online course and will flow more easily into and with course content. Remember our simple rule: collaborative activity is best assessed by collaborative means.

ASSESSMENTS THAT ARE CLEAR AND EASY TO UNDERSTAND

One of the keys to good assessment of collaborative work online is that it be clear, easy to understand, and easy to carry out. For many students, the use of a rubric is daunting. However, if that rubric is constructed with clear, simple language that objectively describes the competencies to be achieved, students should have no difficulty using it to assess themselves and their peers. Likewise, the use of clearly constructed questions, such as the ones we presented earlier in this chapter when discussing self-assessment, can guide students in their thinking and reflection, supporting them to engage meaningfully in assessment. As instructors, we cannot assume that our students will approach the task of assessment from the same perspective as we do or with the same degree of knowledge about what is expected. Therefore, our language needs to be clear and we cannot make assumptions about the understanding of our intent. It can be helpful to create a space on the discussion board of the course where students can feel free to ask questions about the assessment task and clarify information. Prompting students by asking, "Is everyone clear about your assessment task or on how to use the rubric?" will free them up to ask questions that they might otherwise be embarrassed to ask. Furthermore, designing assessment with their input helps to create an assessment process that includes student buy-in and is easier for them to comprehend.

Assessments can be simple and easy to administer. If asking students to write out reflections in the form of a paper or narrative responses to instructor questions seems cumbersome, a simple checklist can be developed that gathers information from students about their collaborative work quickly and easily. One questionnaire can be used throughout the course to assess all collaborative work in a consistent manner. Exhibit 4.2 provides an example of one such questionnaire. Questionnaires can be easily modified to fit more closely with the activity being assessed or to align more closely with course content and learning objectives.

ASSESSMENTS DESIGNED WITH STUDENT INPUT

Learner-focused assessment means inviting the learners to participate in how the assessment is constructed. This method applies as much to exams as to other means of student assessment in a course. One collaborative activity that some instructors have used for constructing tests is to have students submit several test questions as an assignment. The instructor then chooses questions from this student-generated test bank for quizzes or exams. Another way to involve students in designing assessments is to allow a team or small group to determine what they will submit to the instructor to demonstrate team competence at the close of a collaborative activity. In the case of a presentation to the larger group, for example, the students can be left to determine not only what they will present and how they will present it, but the

Exhibit 4.2. Collaboration Questionnaire on Assessment.

Collaboration Factors	Strongly Agree: 1	Somewhat Agree: 2	Neither Agree nor Disagree: 3	Somewhat Disagree: 4	Strongly Disagree: 5
We established common goals.					
We communicated well as a team.					
We chose a leader without difficulty.					
We assigned roles without difficulty.					
Everyone contributed equally to the process.					
Everyone contributed equally to the final product.					
We had adequate time and resources to complete our task.					
I was satisfied with the way we worked together.					
I was satisfied with the final outcome.					
I feel that I learned from this activity.					

Please add any comments below to explain your answers:

"deliverable" that accompanies that presentation as well. Allowing the students the flexibility to produce a presentation, Web page, joint paper, handbook, brochure, or some other artifact that represents their collaborative learning allows them, as Angelo and Cross (1993) contend, to increase their grasp of course concepts. Moreover, it allows for the development of critical thinking skills and creativity within the group. As we often tell groups of faculty when we do faculty training, we are all experts when it comes to our own learning. Respecting that knowledge in designing assessment will help to connect students to the course, the learning process, and one another. It is an important aspect in building an effective learning community.

THE EMPOWERED LEARNER

Byers (2002) states, "The learner-centered environment is widely accepted as the optimum educational paradigm. This paradigm implies that the students themselves are the primary learning resource" (Conclusion, ¶ 2). Clearly, involvement in collaborative activity creates a learner-centered focus that calls for learner-centered assessment, meaning that the student becomes the main resource for and source of assessment information.

The more we engage our students in a process of ongoing evaluation of their own performance, the more meaningful the online course will be to them. The more we engage them in working with one another in both collaborative activity and collaborative assessment, the more likely they are to engage in a learning community that will sustain them beyond the end of the course. The more meaningful the course, the more likely it is that they will become empowered and lifelong learners. Such is the ultimate goal of a constructivist, online classroom that relies on collaboration to engage students in meaning-making and knowledge acquisition, and such is the ultimate value of building a strong online learning community. As one of our learners said to us, learning online is about inclusion, caring, and inquiry. It is a co-constructed learning environment. This is the essence and power of collaboration.

SUMMARY POINTS TO REMEMBER ON ASSESSMENT AND EVALUATION OF COLLABORATIVE WORK

- Collaborative work should be assessed collaboratively.
- Instructors need to provide clear guidelines for assessment of collaborative work.

- The use of rubrics helps to make the assessment task easier and more objective.

- Students need to understand what is expected of them in the assessment function. Providing an area online in which they can clarify this role or ask questions can be helpful.

- When assessment aligns with learning objectives and collaborative activities, the task of assessment becomes less cumbersome and student satisfaction with the learning process increases.

PART
TWO

Collaborative Activities

Role Playing

Role playing is particularly useful in assisting learners to understand the application of concepts. Taking roles helps learners to "take a walk in the shoes" of people they may actually be working with outside of the classroom and gives them practice in a safe situation before engaging in work in the "real world." Involvement with role playing also encourages learners to discover what it means to take a position on a topic—they learn that they need to research the position to determine what a person in that role is likely to say or do as well as to develop their own opinions about potentially controversial topics. Role plays tend to be a hypothetical look at a situation that learners may or may not encounter in their work. Role playing, therefore, can also be used to help develop critical thinking skills as it asks learners to reflect on a situation, discuss it with others, bounce ideas off of others based on what they learn about a particular role, and push them to develop common, consensual solutions to often difficult problems. The following is an example of a role play that could be used with students who are studying or working in health care or as an exercise in the development of critical thinking skills. It presents a controversial situation that requires learners to think in new ways as they consider their own position or role in the situation and then later take the position of a decision maker who is required to offer a solution.

THE SITUATION

Mr. X, a patient at City Hospital, suffers from kidney failure and requires periodic and fairly frequent dialysis, which is funded by the government. He is one of a number of patients who use the dialysis machine, and there are many other similarly afflicted individuals who are on a waiting list for the use of the machine. Mr. X finds dialysis quite painful and sometimes says that he would rather just forget the treatment and let the disease run its natural course. Lately, he has begun to miss some of his appointments for treatment and has been failing to control his diet properly. He has even become abusive with the hospital staff who operate the dialysis machine. His wife is quite worried about him, especially since his behavior has changed toward her and their five children. Mr. X continues his erratic routine, sometimes taking his treatment quietly, sometimes taking it but abusing the staff, and sometimes failing to take it at all. Suddenly, he begins to miss all his treatments. Two weeks later, he is rushed to the hospital in a coma. He must have immediate dialysis if he is to survive. Should the hospital perform the dialysis or should Mr. X be allowed to die?

THE ROLES

Students should discuss this case taking the following assigned roles:

Mr. X's wife
A hospital staff member
Mr. X's doctor
The hospital administrator
Members of the hospital board
A medical ethicist
A representative of the people on the waiting list for dialysis
A member of the "Right to Die" Society

WRITING

After hearing all the arguments presented by the characters in this role play, assume that you are a member of the hospital board that will decide on this case. Write an essay establishing and supporting your position on this issue and share it with the group. Then post comments on the essays of at least two of your team members.

ASSESSMENT TIPS

- Self-assessment by students is appropriate, including what they individually learned by playing the role they did and what they learned about the process as a whole. Self-assessment should include the degree to which the student's participation contributed to the learning of the group.

- Peer assessment of participation of each member of the group and of the essays submitted is appropriate and useful.

Simulations

Simulations are somewhat similar to role playing in that learners are asked to look at what might be a real-life situation and apply concepts and skills learned in class to that situation. What differentiates a simulation from a role play, however, is that a simulation is more closely related to real life and is likely to call for a direct application of skills so as to develop those skills in a work situation. Simulations can be as simple as the discussion example that follows or can take the form of more complicated, software-driven applications that allow students to work through the various stages of a problem or skill in order to master it. Often, software-driven simulations include decision trees, where students can make choices that significantly affect outcomes. These simulations may or may not include group work and involvement. The following is an example of a simple simulation that is easily incorporated into an online course using the discussion board and synchronous communication tools.

DIRECTIONS FOR CASE MANAGEMENT SIMULATION

For this simulation, you have been divided into two treatment teams. The deliberations of both teams are open. Feel free to observe the discussion of the other team, but please only add comments in your own team's discussion.

Each team has been assigned a case to work with. Both cases can be found in Volume Two of your Reader. Team A will work with Don and Team B will work with Jane. The forms that you need to submit at the end of the week are attached to this lesson. Simply click on the filename attached to this lesson to download the file to your computer. The file is in Word format.

First, select a team leader. The team leader will facilitate the discussion and be responsible for submitting the forms to me at the end of the week.

You will note that I will be observing your discussion, but will not get involved in your work. If you hit an impasse or have a question, ask your team leader to e-mail me for my input and I'll post to your discussion. That way, I won't get four or five e-mails on the same topic.

To begin the simulation, each of you should read the case for which you are responsible individually and note the problems you see in the case. You will begin your discussion by posting your individual assessment of the problems in your discussion area, then you'll attempt to come to consensus not only about the problems, but also how they should be coded.

Once you have come up with a team problem list, choose two problems to work with and complete a treatment plan for each of the two problems. Be creative! What kind of specific assignments would you give your client to work with this problem? Please go beyond referral to Twelve-Step meetings, individual and group counseling, and create assignments that stretch you and would also stretch your client. When you agree, have your team leader add that assignment to the treatment plan.

Each team will turn in one problem list and a completed treatment plan to me at the end of the week. This is not a complicated assignment, but because you will be working online and not face-to-face, you will need to be diligent and stay on top of the discussion in order to complete the simulation on time.

Have fun!

ASSESSMENT TIPS

- Self and peer assessment are appropriate and useful with simulations and should include the degree to which participation contributed to the learning of the group.
- More traditional assessment of skill acquisition in the form of tests and quizzes can be used with simulations.

- Authentic evaluation activities, such as those that require the application of the skills learned to a real problem involving the use of the skills, are very appropriate with simulation activities.

Case Studies

Cases may take a variety of forms, but are usually narratives of situations that students are asked to explore critically. Students may also be asked to find and present or create case studies on their own. A case is a true story of organizational issues people have faced, together with facts, opinions, and prejudices on which decisions must be made.

In addition to the narrative, cases may also include charts, graphs, and pictures of relevance to the situation. Case studies vary in length from a few paragraphs to book-chapter length. Some include discussion questions at the end in order to focus the reader's attention on certain issues. Others do not include questions, and part of the reader's challenge is to define the real issues of the case. Cases may be found in casebooks, as sections of textbooks, and on the Internet; cases may be adapted from newspaper and magazine articles, created as fiction, or based on one's own life experience. Anyone can author a case.

With the case method, the process of arriving at an answer is more important than the answer itself. By working through cases, students develop an understanding of the process of reaching decisions and can support and communicate these decisions to others. In this way, cases are similar to role plays and simulations. The following are some guidelines we have previously offered (Palloff and Pratt, 2003) that students can use to begin their analysis of a case study:

1. Read the case rather quickly to get a feel for what is involved.

2. Reread the case and sort out the assumptions, hunches, and facts. Since most cases are incomplete, you can make plausible assumptions about the situation. List those assumptions and be able to support their plausibility. The assumptions enable you to "fill in the blanks" in the case. In organizations, decisions are generally made with incomplete information and some uncertainty.

3. Identify the major problems and subproblems that must be considered in the case. In addition, list the major players in the case and their roles.

4. List the problems in the order of their importance or priority. That is, show which problems must be solved first.

5. Develop a list of alternative courses of action that minimize or eliminate the problems. If possible, have at least two fully developed alternatives that are feasible solutions.

6. In developing alternative courses of action, outline the constraints (such as resources, historical precedent, competition, skill limitations, attitudes) that limit success.

7. Select the best course of action for the problems identified in step three. Show how the course of action would work and be able to discuss why it would be the most successful alternative for solving the problems.

The following is an example of a case used in an organizational behavior course that encourages students to apply course readings and discussions to a work situation.

THE AROMA CHOCOLATE COMPANY

The Aroma Chocolate Company was founded thirty years ago. At the time of its founding, the company created a "family-like" culture. The company consisted of a chocolate factory and initially one retail outlet. The company prided itself on the production of a very dark, aromatic chocolate that appealed to the chocolate connoisseur. Over the years the company grew to thirty-one retail outlets and recently moved its factory into a larger plant.

Although employees have not been paid a great deal to work in the stores, they traditionally expressed high levels of satisfaction related to the emphasis on training programs, the provision of health benefits (which is unusual in retail settings of this kind), and the accessibility of upper management. Employees felt included and involved in decisions affecting the company and heard by upper management. Moreover, store management was team oriented. Employees also enjoyed the company-sponsored activities, such as picnics and holiday parties. Moreover, they looked forward to receiving an annual holiday bonus as well as gifts from the company, such as T-shirts and coffee mugs decorated with the company logo, as well as the ability to take home samples weekly. It was not uncommon for employees to work in the retail outlets for fifteen years or more.

About ten years after the company began operation, a small group of employees left to start another company, Moon and Stars Chocolate, in another state. The Aroma Company assisted them by providing training for Moon and Stars employees and sharing employees between the two firms. Shortly, however, Moon and Stars developed and implemented a new strategy involving rapid growth, a national chain of retail stores, and a strong marketing push to support the growth. In addition, they developed low carb and low fat chocolates that were more appealing to the general public. Because of the growing interest in eating gourmet candy and in weight loss, the concept caught on, and Moon and Stars soon became well known and very successful.

Aroma had no desire to expand into a national market and reaffirmed their strategy to maintain the high quality of chocolate they had always produced and to keep their emphasis on customer service in their existing stores. Soon, however, they began to feel the competition from Moon and Stars. Senior management became concerned about a reduction in market share and lower profits. Some of the people in management positions were asked to leave and new managers were hired who had experience working in large retail companies. Several new strategies were put in place, including rapidly opening new retail outlets and reducing staffing hours, with increased hours of operation. More part-time staff were hired with no possibility of earning benefits due to the number of hours worked weekly. The annual holiday bonus was awarded only to stores with the highest level of sales during the holiday season. Training programs were cut back. The annual picnic was eliminated, as were the free T-shirts and mugs for employees. Employees could purchase these items if they desired.

The results of these strategies were less than positive. Store managers began to leave the company, causing senior management to offer each store manager bonuses of up to 25 percent of the manager's salary based on store sales. The store managers were concerned that the bonuses did not apply to the other members of the management team at the store level. A recent employee survey revealed declining overall job satisfaction and a feeling that management has shifted to a top-down model, allowing for little employee input into decision making.

In your small group, discuss the following questions and present your group responses to the larger class on Friday:

1. Evaluate this case using Gareth Morgan's contingency model.
2. How congruent are this company's values and actions? Explain.
3. Appraise management's handling of the problems in this case. What behavioral ideas were overlooked or misapplied?
4. What are the key problems in this case? What organizational ideas discussed in class would you apply to deal with these problems?

ASSESSMENT TIPS

- Instructor-generated cases can be assessed through the questions asked of students in response to the case. In addition, instructors can assess how well course concepts were addressed and incorporated into the review and analysis of the case.
- Students can be asked to identify not only the concepts applied, but also any new knowledge that was generated by working on the case study.

STUDENT-GENERATED CASES

Case studies need not be generated by the instructor. A collaborative technique that works well online is to encourage students to bring case studies from their own work or life situations into the online classroom and to receive input from their peers on potential solutions. The following are two ways to present a similar assignment so students can generate their own cases and ways the group can work on those cases collaboratively.

CASE STUDY PREPARATION

Provide a general description of a problem or issue you would like to work on. This can be related to a work project or problem that you have been asked to address that involves e-training or the development of a virtual work team. Or it can be related to the development of an online course or training session in any setting. Discuss the following in your presentation:

What are the specific issues in this case? What would you like help with?
How are some of the issues we have been reading about and discussing reflected here?
What are some initial ideas you have about this case or situation?

Cases should be one or two pages in length. Please give each other feedback and engage in some discussion about the case! Please remember our guideline of confidentiality as we post and discuss these cases!

COLLABORATIVE WORK ON CASES

Together you will choose four cases that you would like to discuss and develop more thoroughly. Your task will be to provide feedback on the issues outlined and provide solutions to any problems or concerns based on our reading and discussion. Depending on the number of students enrolled in the course, collaborative small groups may work on a case together and present the agreed-upon solution to the larger group. The small groups will negotiate their presentation date to the large group. If numbers enrolled in the course are smaller, we will discuss with you how you would like to work on and present cases. All decisions about collaborative casework and presentations will be made during Week Six of the course.

COLLABORATIVE DESIGN PROJECT

In Week Six, each of you will be asked to post a brief case study of approximately one to two paragraphs in length describing a situation involving either an existing virtual team that is in need of further development or that is experiencing issues or problems, or a situation where virtual team work should or could be used. We will choose two of those cases and divide into two smaller working teams to develop them during Weeks Nine, Ten, and Eleven. The design project must incorporate the concepts and theory that we have been reading about and discussing. The final product from the two groups will be a project plan that can be reviewed and discussed by the full class.

ASSESSMENT TIPS

- Instructors can develop a rubric or assessment matrix outlining course concepts and mapping the student case presentation to those concepts.

- Students can assess themselves as to whether their case addresses course concepts, what they learned about course material from preparing the case, and any additional learning from working on the case with their group.

Questioning Techniques for Collaborative Discussions

We cannot forget that discussion of course material on the discussion board of an online course constitutes collaborative activity. As learners interact with one another to explore the territory that comprises the course, they engage in a constructivist process of collaborative knowledge generation that can result in community building, the development of critical thinking skills, and deeper understanding of the material being studied. The instructor can assist in this process by providing good discussion questions that guide students' thinking and interaction with one another. In *Discussion as a Way of Teaching*, Brookfield and Preskill (1999) offer several categories of questions to stimulate and maintain discussion. We offered these previously in *The Virtual Student* (2003), but offer them again here as a means of stimulating thinking about the types of questions that can foster collaboration. The following is a summary and digest of the categories and questions along with suggestions for their use to assist instructors in creating discussion questions for an online course:

> *Questions that ask for more evidence.* This category of questions can assist learners in developing higher levels of critical thinking and in taking a position, as is needed in the completion of role-play activities.

They can also be used to guide the feedback that learners give one another as they complete their collaborative work on assignments.

- How do you know that?
- What data is that claim based on?
- What do others say that support your argument?
- Where did you find that view expressed in the materials?
- What evidence would you give to someone who doubted your interpretation?

Questions that ask for clarification. This category of questions is especially useful as feedback questions for learners to use with one another as they complete collaborative assignments. These questions assist learners in getting clear on their thinking and presenting their ideas in a cogent manner.

- Can you put that another way?
- What's a good example of what you are talking about?
- What do you mean by that?
- Can you explain the term you just used?
- Could you give a different illustration of your point?

Open-ended questions. The use of open-ended questions can stimulate interaction in an online discussion. They encourage learners to dig deeper when responding to material and to go beyond answers that are comprised of just a few words. The responses to these questions can provide the "meat" of a course as the questions encourage learners to bring in resources beyond what might be assigned reading in order to respond fully.

- Sauvage says that when facing moral crises, people who agonize don't act, and people who act don't agonize. What does this mean? (Follow-up question: Can you think of an example that is consistent with Sauvage's maxim and another that conflicts with it?)

- Racism pervaded American society throughout the twentieth century. What are some signs that racial discrimination still exists in hiring? What are other signs that racism has abated significantly?
- Why do you think many people devote their lives to education despite the often low pay and poor working conditions?

Linking or extension questions. Linking and extension questions help to develop the themes that are emerging in an online discussion. They can be used to help learners see connections they might otherwise be missing and to move the discussion to a deeper level as those connections are explored more fully.

- How does your comment fit in with Neng's earlier comment?
- How does your observation relate to what the group decided last week?
- Does your idea challenge or support what we seem to be saying?
- How does that contribution add to what has already been said?

Hypothetical questions. Hypothetical questions form the foundation of role play, simulation, and case study activities. In order to engage with these activities fully, learners should wrestle with "what if" types of questions that are designed to stimulate reflection and possibilities.

- If you were presented with the following question in an interview, how would you respond: "Was your previous job full of purposeful play or drudgery and work?"
- You have only two years to live and will do so with your usual energy and vitality. What will you do with your last two years?
- You just won a $100 million lottery jackpot. What will you do with the rest of your life?

Cause-and-effect questions. Cause-and-effect questions, if designed well, can be very useful in exploring case studies. They push learners to look at potential scenarios and possible solutions.

- What is likely to be the effect of changing from a one-to-one mode of working to a group mode?
- How might delivering our courses using the Internet affect our students' learning process?

Summary and synthesis questions. Summary and synthesis questions are particularly important when reflecting on and evaluating a collaborative activity. They not only allow learners to look at what they have accomplished through their work together, but also assist them in determining where there may be some gaps in their learning and what more they might need to pursue in order to grasp the material fully.

- What are the one or two most important ideas that emerged from this discussion?
- What remains unresolved or contentious about this topic?
- What do you understand better as a result of today's discussion?
- Based on our discussion today, what do we need to talk about next time if we're to understand this issue better?

ASSESSMENT TIPS

- Contributions to online discussions can be assessed using the following basic guidelines:

Synthesis and Integration = A

Analysis = B

Summary = C

- Assessment of discussions should include the student's contribution through their initial response to the discussion questions as well as their substantive responses to other students. Substantive responses can be defined as follows:

Comments critically or analytically to another post

Begins a new topic

Asks another question

Dyads

In our own experience of working with collaboration in online classes, we have found the use of dyads to be a particularly powerful tool; it is easily accommodated by most learners and helps to build a bridge to collaborative group work either later in the course or in other courses. By beginning with dyads, learners are able to form a partnership that provides them with support in their learning. Through dyad work, learners can bounce their ideas off of another person, helping to shape and develop them. Dyad work also helps learners to develop an appreciation of the value of collaboration. We tend to see less resistance to collaborative assignments when the learner is expected to work with only one other person. A gradual shift to larger group work becomes easier as a result; for example, by pairing dyads into a group of four.

There are some caveats in dyad formation, however. The instructor should pay attention to the following when forming dyads:

- *Time zone issues.* Learners often complain about an inability to connect with a partner in a distant time zone. Pairing learners within the same time zone or with minimal time zone differences can remove this barrier to communication.

- *Performance levels in the course.* It is a good idea to wait a week or two to see how learners are engaging with the course discussions before forming dyads. In so doing, strategic pairings can be made to encourage a learner who may be lagging, for example, by pairing that learner with one who is keeping up with course assignments. However, an instructor may also choose to pair learners who are both either participating at a high or low level to minimize frustration in the completion of collaborative work.

• *Work or educational situations.* One of us experienced a problem with a random pairing of learners in an online class. One learner was a vice president in a large corporation while the other was a single mother. The corporate vice president was intolerant of the connection difficulties experienced by the single mother and lashed out at her in anger, suggesting that she needed to buy a laptop computer in order to be successful in the course and program. The single mother, who was struggling to pay tuition and feed her children at the same time, was very upset by this lack of sensitivity to her situation. The instructor needed to intervene to help these learners become more sensitive to one another and to enable them to complete the assigned activity.

• *Self-selection of partner.* Allowing learners to select their own partners can help to alleviate the concerns with dyad formation. However, what can ensue is "fourth grade syndrome," wherein one learner is left out of the selection process. Furthermore, if learners are expected to select their own partners, additional time for the collaborative activity must be allowed so that the selection process can occur. The following checklist can be helpful for partner selection:

- Read the introductions or profiles of your fellow learners and look for similar interests, locations, hobbies, or anything else that might connect you.
- Are you in the same time zone? Is that important to you?
- Are you in the same general geographic location? Is that important to you?
- Are issues of gender, culture, or educational level important to you?
- Evaluate your potential partner's posts to the discussion—do you share ideas, concepts, desires, or beliefs?
- Do you share at about the same level and seem to care about similar things?
- Are your participation levels about equal?
- Do you seem to share similar expectations for the course?

The following are two examples of dyad activities for an online course. In one, learners are asked to select a partner. In the other, the instructor forms dyads.

DYAD ACTIVITY: FIND AND WORK WITH A PARTNER

Find one other learner in the course whose interests are close enough to yours that you can work together as a dyad (a two-person team). Use your analysis of previous postings and your review of student profiles to make your choice. Communicate by telephone or e-mail to establish your working relationship, then carry out the following activity together:

- Share with your new partner the results of your previous Internet searches.

- Select one or two sources that you both agree will provide relevant information on how educational theory has affected the development of the issues you *both* are examining. Add to your analysis the ideas you gleaned from the two chapters you read in the text.

- Use the results of your interaction to prepare a joint posting to the discussion board based on your search and analysis. It should discuss how your two issues share common historical roots and represent different theoretical perspectives.

DYAD ACTIVITY: ASSIGNED PARTNERS

Your instructor will assign you a dyad partner. Meet with your partner in the on-line classroom and, first, give yourselves a name so that you can find each other easily. With your partner, discuss a workplace or professional problem you think you might like to address. Do an Internet or library search to find two or three references that address this problem and share the ideas you have found with your partner. What does the literature say about the problem you have identified?

Meet with your partner in the online classroom and discuss ways in which you might address the problem you identified in Unit Six and wrote about in Unit Seven. What is the problem you are addressing? How do you think you can address this problem? What changes will need to be made? What forms and strategies of change will need to be employed? Provide an outline of what you think will be an effective change process and give one another feedback on your plans.

ASSESSMENT TIPS

- Participation on an equal level is an important assessment factor for dyads as is the quality of work or discussions produced.
- Self-assessment and assessment of the dyad partner are appropriate, but should be done in the form of a private message to the instructor.

Small-Group Projects

The use of small groups is one of the most commonly accepted forms of collaborative activity in any course, whether face-to-face or online. Incorporating small groups into an online course allows for deeper involvement with aspects of the course and helps to reduce possible information overload by minimizing the number of other students with whom one student communicates. Small-group projects encourage learners to expand their work and thinking by working with others, allow learners to engage deeply on a topic within the course, and give them the chance to work with a team to produce a common piece of work. Certainly, virtual teaming is part of the completion of a small-group project, as are other forms of collaborative activity, but it is the focus on the collaboratively created deliverable that differentiates small-group projects from simply working in a virtual team. The following is an example of a small-group project taken from an undergraduate class entitled the History of American Business.

D O I N G   B U S I N E S S   I N   T H E   U S A !

Your main deliverable for this course in the History of American Business will be to work in small groups to develop and present the history and significance of a specific industry that we will be reading about. Each topic has an assigned week in the syllabus. During the first and second weeks of class, I will ask you to post your interests in the topics to the discussion board. We will form groups based on interest. The industries your group can elect to present on are one of the following:

Agribusiness and transportation
Banking and insurance
Marketing and retailing
Multinationals and high tech

As you work in your small groups, consider the following for your presentations:

- Each member of the group is expected to contribute a significant piece to the preparation and delivery of the presentation. How you decide who will do what is up to you, but you will be submitting an evaluation of your own and your team members' participation and contributions after you present, so contributing equally is of benefit to all!
- You may want to choose a leader to guide your process and to make sure that all work is completed according to a schedule and on time.
- Make it interesting and fun! Send us on a Web quest, create a game for us to play, use graphics, give us some assignments to complete—whatever you do, make sure that it goes well beyond "read the assignment and answer these questions." The week prior to your presentation, you are free to assign some preliminary work to the remainder of the class so that we are prepared for your presentation. This work can include additional reading or visits to appropriate Web sites—it's up to the group!
- Remember that your presentation is not just a chronological report on your industry. We can all read that in the textbook! Instead, your presentation should bring that history to life somehow and illustrate its significance in American history and in the world of business today.

ASSESSMENT TIPS

- Small-group projects demand self-assessment on the part of individuals to determine the quality of their contributions to the group. Also, asking each group member to assess every other group member can be helpful to the instructor.
- Consider assigning individual grades based on individual contributions to the group as well as a group grade for the final product.

Jigsaw Activities

Jigsaw activities are a good way to expand the content presented in an online course by asking learners to become experts in an area and present that area to their peers either directly or by contributions to a larger group project. In so doing, learners complete the "puzzle" of the content being explored and add to the knowledge of each member of the group. Jigsaw activities can play a significant role in solidifying the theory an instructor wants to present by sending learners in search of material and bringing it back to the group. In addition, as mentioned in the previous section, jigsaw activities can be the process students use to complete a small-group project. The following is an example of such an activity.

Introduction. The work of the early theorists has stood the test of time. For example, action research is still fundamental for all organizational development (OD) work. And even today, Theory X and Theory Y can be used to understand a manager's approach. But our field is just as subject to the current turbulent environment as every other. Further, our understanding of human and organizational systems is a work in progress. So the question is not, "What has been abandoned or found wrong?" Rather, it is "What has been added?" A list of current topics having an impact on OD is provided below. You will each explore one topic and then educate the rest of us on that topic as it affects OD. All papers will be posted during one unit. You will then have the opportunity to engage in discussion with the author of the paper for an additional week.

Assignment. Please write and post a paper on your selected topic. Inform us about the topic, being sure to answer the following: How does what is going on in each of these areas affect OD? What does it mean for the field of OD and for OD practitioners? How does it affect the connection between human systems and organizational structures and processes? (Length: 2,000 words; decide together who will work on each topic.)

C U R R E N T   T O P I C S :

- Working with adaptive systems (chaos and complexity theory applied to organizations)
- Creating inclusivity; ameliorating oppression (diversity in the workplace)
- Dialogue (building authentic collaboration and trust; bridging the communication gap)
- New economy and next economy (Internet and other technological advances; ever-increasing need for speed; geographically dispersed teams; but also could include OD issues for start-ups as well as dot-com meltdowns, and so on)
- Learning communities and organizational learning
- Knowledge management
- Merged cultures, globalization of an organization

**Remember: How does what is going on in each of these areas affect *OD*? What does it mean for the field of OD and for OD practitioners?

How does it affect the connection between human systems and organizational structures and processes?

ASSESSMENT TIPS

- Jigsaw activities create a unique opportunity for peer as well as instructor review. Peer review might take the form of the following questions:

What were the strengths of this paper?

How did this paper contribute to your own learning?

How might it have been improved?

- A reflective self-assessment is also appropriate regarding jigsaw contributions.

Blogs

A blog, or Web log, is a personal Web site updated frequently with links, commentary, and anything else someone chooses to post there. New items go on top and older items flow down the page. Bloggers are encouraged to throw their ideas into their blogs as they occur. The blog form is unique to the Web and is often used for developing community in the online world. Originating in journalism, blogs are a relatively new addition to online courses and can be used as course journals or personal diaries; they can focus on one narrow subject or range across a number of topics. Students can be encouraged to create collaborative blogs, adding to and commenting on preceding topics. What makes a blog different from a threaded discussion is that the entries are not in response to discussion questions, but are free-flowing ideas that emerge from the material being studied. In this way, students can collaboratively reflect on material, brainstorm, and move far outside of the confines of assigned text or resource material in their thinking. Blogging can be used as a way to capture student reflections on content throughout an online course or during a virtual team or small-group activity.

Blood's *Weblog Handbook* (2002) provides six guidelines for blogging that can be used to steer students in creating a blog in a course:

1. Publish as fact only that which you believe to be true.

2. If material exists online, link to it when you reference it.

3. Publicly correct any misinformation.

4. Write each entry as if it could not be changed; add to, but do not rewrite or delete any entry.

5. Disclose any conflict of interest.

6. Note questionable and biased sources. (Weblog Ethics, ¶ 10)

The following is one way in which blogging could be used in an online course as part of a small-group assignment.

K E E P   A   B L O G !

As you gather research on your topic of interest, throw some of that material into a "blog" or Web log that you and your group members can refer and add to. Your ideas do not have to be well formed. It's more a way to brainstorm as you find new material to consider. In this way, you and your group will be creating a joint reflective journal that you can refer to later when you complete your collaborative paper or project. Make sure to keep the ethical guidelines for blogging, as presented in the syllabus, in mind as you add your entries. Remember that there will be five of you looking at and using your entries, so even though these are brainstorms and reflections, you want them to reflect accurate material and interpretation of facts. You can choose to open your blog to other groups or keep it private for your own group only. Please inform the larger group of your decision in this regard.

ASSESSMENT TIPS

- Blogs are not often assessed, as they represent brainstorms that contribute to group learning or the completion of a group project.

- If assessment occurs, it should be on participation and not necessarily on the contribution itself.

Virtual Teams

Virtual team activities help to bring learners together to sort out problems and engage in deeper discussion. Given that many business and educational organizations now employ virtual teams as an integral part of how the work gets accomplished, working on virtual teams allows students to experience what it might be like to work in a distributed work situation. Virtual teaming can be used to create small discussion groups, as part of a simulation, or in the completion of a small-group project. In fact, virtual teams are extensively used in many online courses in many forms. The following example illustrates how a simulated virtual team can be used so that students can experience team formation and team process and also complete a collaborative project. The assessment of this activity would include a review of how well the team worked together and what the group learned about virtual teams by being a part of one.

This is a team assignment based on Sproull and Kiesler's *Connections: New Ways of Working in the Networked Organization* (1992) and the journal articles assigned for the course. You are asked to consider the influence and impact of technology and electronic communications on group behavior.

1. Imagine that you are a member of a consulting team developing a proposal to a client organization.

2. Choose an issue introduced in the readings that relates to your work setting.

3. How would you design and implement a structure or process within your organization that reflects your understanding of this issue?

   (Note: You will probably not be able to identify an issue that is directly relevant to the work situations of all your team members. Try to choose a topic that will have some relevance for as many of your group as possible.)

4. As a consulting group, write an eight-page proposal (3,000 words) to respond to this issue. Begin the paper by briefly evaluating the current state of knowledge about this topic. Then provide a little background to the problem or opportunity to the organization. Finally, offer your proposal. This is a group project with a single, final posting from the entire group. You will have to work out your own processes regarding roles, leadership, decision-making, and so on. However, *all* of your communication with one another on this assignment must be done electronically through the discussion forum; through synchronous chat, should you choose to use it; and, conceivably, via e-mail. You are also required to copy me on any messages that you send to the group or to any member of the group relating to this assignment and at least let me know when a chat session will be occurring—I may choose to attend or you can invite me to attend should you have a specific concern that you'd like to work out in my presence. You have three weeks to complete the assignment.

ASSESSMENT TIPS

- As with small-group projects, virtual teams demand self-assessment on the part of individuals to determine the quality of their contributions to the group. Also, asking each group member to assess every other group member can be helpful to the instructor.

- Consider assigning individual grades based on individual contributions to the group as well as a group grade for the final product.

- Make sure to assess the team's process by asking each member to reflect on how they tackled their task, assigned roles, moved through the process to completion, and so forth. Team members will learn a great deal about working in virtual teams by reflecting on their own process.

Debates

Debates can be a lively and fun way to help learners engage with one another, while raising the level of critical thinking in the course by pushing students to prepare material to support their own position and to evaluate the positions of others. Just as in face-to-face classes, debates can be conducted by having individuals debate one another on ideas and positions or by having teams prepare for and engage in debate. Debate activities can involve asking students to take on roles or asking them to engage in a fictitious dialogue and debate with one of the authors of the book they are reading or one or more of the critical theorists who have contributed to the body of knowledge being studied. There are a couple of important points to remember when preparing a debate activity: First, set it up around a topic that is just controversial enough to allow students to take a position but not so controversial that it may result in flaming, or personal attacks. Second, establish rules and guidelines for debate in advance in order to keep communication professional and on target. The following example provides instructions for a sample debate.

Place yourself in one of the following roles:

- Attorney for a teachers' union
- State legislator who oversees education
- Institution chief executive (superintendent or college president)
- Journalist who covers education for a local newspaper

You have been asked to take part in a public debate on the topic "Resolved: Financing education is *not* the responsibility of the society." You have a choice of whether to be on the *pro* side or on the *con* side, and your job is to write a 300- to 500-word position statement that does the following:

- Provides the historical and sociocultural background to the debate.
- Presents the major arguments in support of the pro or con position you have taken.
- Presents answers to the challenges you expect from the opposing position.

Post on the discussion board the role you plan to take and the position (pro or con) on the issue to be debated. Then present your position paper to the group.

Respond to one or two learners whose position(s) you disagree with and engage in a mini-debate in which you exchange at least three ideas. Following the debate, prepare a final post indicating whether or not your position on the issue has changed as the result of the debate, noting why and how.

ASSESSMENT TIPS

- Ask students to reflect on their learning from participating in the debate and to evaluate the activity as a learning activity.
- Instructors can easily assess individual contributions to a debate if individual students are debating other students.
- The use of debate teams complicates the process a bit. In this case, self-assessment and peer assessments help the instructor to determine levels of participation and contributions to the team's debate position.

Fishbowls

Fishbowl activities allow students to practice a skill while being observed by others. The idea is to provide a safe container where mistakes can be made and performance critiqued in a professional and supportive way. Fishbowls can be set up with a small group interacting with the instructor or the group simply interacting with one another around skill development, while the remaining students observe. Critical to the success of fishbowl activities is that the observing students not share their reflections right away, but give the students in the fishbowl an opportunity to demonstrate what they know. Being silent and observing are important skills taught through this exercise and ones that active, engaged learners may have some difficulty mastering. Learners often note that it is more difficult to be outside the fishbowl observing than it is being a member of the group being observed. They may even express frustration with the process and find difficulty in understanding what is gained by observation. It becomes the instructor's role to ensure that the sanctity of the fishbowl is maintained and to process those frustrations and questions at the appropriate time to help achieve the desired outcomes. The following is an example of a fishbowl activity used to help students learn how to facilitate an online group.

> You will participate in a group-facilitation "fishbowl" activity in Units Five through Eight. Groups of five will be established by the instructor(s) and each group will be assigned a unit that they will be responsible for discussing and facilitating. Each member of the group is expected to facilitate for one day while

the remainder of the group participates in the discussion. During the fourth week of the course, each group is responsible for communicating with their group members to determine who will take responsibility for facilitation on what day of the assigned week. That group will, in essence, be in the "fishbowl" while the remaining learners are responsible to be key observers of the process. There will be a discussion topic created where the remaining learners can ask process-oriented questions, such as, "John, don't you feel that your question could have been better worded to elicit a stronger response?" The last day of each discussion week will be a debriefing session for all learners. The instructor will also act as an observer and will provide a summary of the reflections of the observer group as well as an evaluation of the group in the fishbowl at the end of each week. The instructor will also interact with the groups that are not in the fishbowl in the discussion area for reflections. Discussion of the previous week's reflections will likely be occurring at the same time that the facilitation for the current week is happening. We will repeat this process in Units Five through Eight.

This is clearly an intensive process and requires that the group in the fishbowl be online everyday during their facilitation week. The observers need to check in at least three times during the week and also need to keep a journal of observations in order to debrief effectively at the end of each week. You will be very tempted, as an observer, to jump into the discussion. The journal, therefore, will also assist you in maintaining your "silence" as you observe during each week.

ASSESSMENT TIPS

- Fishbowl activities can be somewhat tricky to assess. The instructor can observe the activities of the group in the fishbowl and assess those directly, but the observations of the remaining members of the group may be difficult to determine. Having the observers turn in their weekly journals as well as posting reflections that are evaluated by the instructor can alleviate this difficulty.

- Observers should be encouraged not only to reflect on what they observed during the week, but also to assess the performance of the group in the fishbowl, either through their posted observations or through weekly e-mails or private messages to the instructor.

Learning Cycles

Learning cycles are sets of activities that are most often used to tap into various learning styles in a class. Learning cycles are also a good way to incorporate many forms of collaborative activity into the completion of a larger project that might span the better part of a term. Learning cycles occur in phases. Each phase contains an activity that is organized around a theme or problem, with the emphasis on the development of a skill set. Once that skill set is mastered, students can move on to the next phase of activity. In essence, learning cycles are a means by which learners can scaffold their learning. A simulation, for example, that spans several units in a course might incorporate learning cycles. In each unit, the group may be mastering and demonstrating relevant skills together before moving on to the next unit. If the assignment is for a group of students to build a database or Web page together, for example, each unit may teach the group a skill that they will need to work toward completion of the project. In this way, highly complex projects can be built by teams as the course progresses and presented as a final project. The following is an example of a collaborative learning cycle.

COLLABORATIVE DESIGN PROJECT

In Week Six, each of you will be asked to post a brief case study, approximately one to two paragraphs in length, describing one of two situations: an existing virtual team that is in need of further development or is experiencing issues or problems, or a situation in which virtual teamwork should or could be utilized. We will choose two of those cases and divide into two smaller working teams to develop them during Weeks Nine, Ten, and Eleven into a design project. The design project must incorporate the concepts and theory we have been reading about and discussing. The final product from each of the two groups will be a model for virtual teaming that can be reviewed and discussed by the full class. Models can include graphic representations, organizational charts, role and position descriptions, and any other written material that will assist the other team in understanding the model.

The projects will follow a process in which pieces will be added to the final design each week based on the readings and discussion topics for that week. The process will be as follows:

Week Six: This week will focus on start-up. Reading for Week Six is on start-up factors. Please post a case study idea by Wednesday that you would like to see the group work on. The large group will choose two cases to develop and will divide into teams based on interest in the cases chosen. The model for virtual teaming to be developed will be based on the reading in class, any additional resources brought in by team members, and team discussion. Models must include and address the topics we will discuss in Weeks Seven and Eight.

Weeks Seven and Eight: Reading and discussion will be on the following topics:

- Inputs, processes, outputs (as a model)
- Information management (access, process, store, retrieve, utilize)
- Work-process management (meetings, action plans, telephone calls, face-to-face discussion, and so forth)
- Process facilitation
- Goal setting
- Coaching
- Training (technical, business, relationship)

During Weeks Seven and Eight, teams will meet in small-group discussion to begin preparation of their project design. You may choose to appoint a leader and any other roles that you feel will be necessary to complete the project.

Week Nine: The teams will focus on demonstrating mastery of the following issues in your team project design by responding to the following questions:

What is your initial model for virtual team development (including inputs, processes, and outputs)?
How might you display this graphically?
How will your virtual team manage information?
How will your virtual team manage work processes?

Teams will present their models to one another by Friday of Week Nine.
Week Ten: The teams will add to their models by demonstrating mastery of the following skills:

- Process facilitation

- Goal setting

- Coaching

- Training

Teams will present their further developed models to one another by Friday of Week Ten.
Week Eleven: The teams will prepare their final projects and present them to one another by Friday of Week Eleven, focusing on organizational implementation and including reflections on group process and the group product. Questions for reflection will be posted on the discussion board.

Another means by which to accomplish learning cycles is to let the resources used guide the process. If the reading pushes learners to higher levels of skill development, it can be used to guide collaborative process. The following simple dyad activity, based on *Leadership from the Inside Out* (Cashman, 1998), is an example.

Your instructor will post a schedule of dyad assignments. You will be assigned a partner with whom you will reflect on the Cashman Pathways beginning with Unit Two. Each of the seven pathways will push you to deeper levels of reflection on your skills. Your reflections on the pathways should be approximately one page and should be drawn from the work you did on each of the exercises you completed while reading the pathway. You do not need to report the results of the exercises to your dyad partner unless you choose to, but instead should reflect on the totality of your responses and what they mean to you. At the end of each unit, either you or your partner will provide a collaborative report on your discussion to the larger group. Make sure to decide weekly on who will report out.

ASSESSMENT TIPS

- Regardless of the form of learning cycle used, assessment of the activities should occur at the end of each cycle so that students can learn from the previous round and make adjustments accordingly.

- There should be regular reporting out from small groups to the larger group as each learning cycle is completed. The reporting should include lessons learned from the activity, new skills developed, and how those skills are being applied either in real-world situations or in relationship to the course.

WebQuests

WebQuests are an increasingly popular technological form of a scavenger hunt. They can be a fun and exciting way to promote collaborative exploration of a topic and can incorporate many forms of collaborative activity. Often WebQuests scaffold knowledge acquisition through a series of tasks that comprise learning cycles. Each learning cycle addresses different components of the whole. For example, the first cycle may involve researching the topic, the second cycle might consist of evaluating the material obtained by visiting Web sites devoted to evaluation, and the third cycle might be producing an artifact, paper, or project that incorporates the first two cycles. WebQuests can be designed in a number of ways, with some suggested here.

• Students can be asked to form teams to search out components of a concept that collectively form a complete view of the concept when they are done. For example, a group of technology students might go on a journey to build a computer by finding information about each component they might need and then document the reasons for their choices.

• Students can be asked to take roles and search out a topic in role. For example, business students could be given a case study about a bank failure. Roles would be assigned and students would then search out appropriate information on the Internet that would allow them to work the case together. The instructor could provide links to material that he or she particularly wants the students to review in their quest.

• Teams of students can be given a quest, such as to visit and evaluate various programs in order to build one of their own. An example might be to visit Web sites of education programs devoted to working with student learning styles, evaluate those programs by visiting evaluation sites, and then build an "ideal" program based on the information gathered in both phases of the quest. The following is an example of a WebQuest designed to encourage students to develop good Internet search skills and the ability to evaluate Web sites. It was developed and contributed by Richard Graham, MLS, of Texas A&M University. (Note: italicized words in the following text refer to linked primers on the topics that are part of the course presentation; references to Dr. Martin Luther King Jr. are sites on the World Wide Web.)

Not all information or sources of information are created equal. This is particularly true of Web sites.

As more people gain access to information on the Web and more content is continuously added, it is important to know how to evaluate Web sites to determine if the information found is reliable. Most Web content is posted without any form of review, so it is up to you to make sure that the information you find is credible. Some embarrassing *mistakes* have occurred when authors neglected to apply scrutiny to online information.

Web pages exist for different reasons: some are designed as *marketing tools* or for more *subversive reasons,* while others are meant to entertain. They may offer *news* or may be for *satire.* While there certainly is excellent information to be found online—especially through our *government* or *library* databases—the trouble may be accessing it freely, or knowing where and how to search.

Are you an expert at locating reliable information online? Do you know how to determine who is responsible for the content you are about to use for your research paper?

Y O U R   Q U E S T

Become an expert user of online information. Explore the criteria often used to evaluate Web sources and share your expertise with your classmates.

Task 1

In this WebQuest you will be working with two teams of students in your class. The first team will consist of five members and you will explore the background information provided and try to answer the related questions together.

Task 2

In your next task, you will either assume an expert role or be assigned one (either accuracy, authority, coverage, currency, or objectivity). You will then meet with other participants of like roles to form a new group and work together on a five- to ten-minute presentation.

Group 1: All accuracy
Group 2: All authority
Group 3: All coverage
Group 4: All currency
Group 5: All objectivity

In your presentations you will go over Web sites you've discovered using provided search tools and demonstrate how to apply your group's criterion to online information.

Your group is expected to have visuals such as a poster, video, photographs, or a PowerPoint slide show as part of your demonstration. All team members of your group are expected to be a part of the presentation. You will also be expected to answer questions (if any) from the class. Submit either an outline or the presentation (if in PowerPoint) to your teacher upon the completion of the project in person or via e-mail.

Task 3

Your third task is to regroup with your original team and discover Web sites and online information according to a topic of your choice using search tools of your choice. Your team will then give a fifteen- to twenty-minute presentation of your findings.

In your group presentation, you will be expected to rank your Web pages according to reliability. You will also need to explain what search tools you used and why. This is in addition to demonstrating applications of all criteria to each page.

Again, your group is expected to have visuals such as a poster, video, photographs, or a PowerPoint slide show. All team members of your group are expected to be a part of the presentation and be prepared for questions or discussion. Submit either an outline or the presentation (if in PowerPoint) to your teacher upon the completion of the project in person or via e-mail.

THE PROCESS

1. You will form a team of five students and you will explore the provided Web sites. While doing so, try to answer these basic questions together:

- Who owns, manages, or writes the content for these sites?

- Would you use either of these Web sites for a paper, and why or why not?

- What is the purpose for each Web site? In other words, is it intended to persuade, inform, or sell you something?

Martin Luther King Jr.—A True Historical Examination
The Martin Luther King Jr. Papers Project
Take notes and be prepared to discuss your experiences with the rest of the class.

2. You will next split up into expert roles, each assuming a criterion to explore (accuracy, authority, coverage, currency, or objectivity) and form new teams consisting of fellow experts (all accuracy experts, all authority experts, and so forth). Each expert group will look at provided Web sites to discuss listed questions. The group will then use assigned search tools to locate Web sites of their own and apply the given criterion. These will also be the Web sites used for the class presentation. Before you go searching, you may want to visit the brief primers on basic Web *design* and *URLs*.

Your presentation must last between five and ten minutes, and must include visuals, preferably as a PowerPoint show or iMovie, but posters, pictures, and screen shots will suffice. All members must participate and be prepared for any discussion or questions. You may want to review the *Rubrics* page to see exactly what's expected for your presentation. Submit an outline or the presentation (if PowerPoint, iMovie, or Flash) upon completion of the project in person or via e-mail.

Group 1: Accuracy
Group 2: Authority
Group 3: Coverage
Group 4: Currency
Group 5: Objectivity

3. After your first presentations, you will next regroup with your original team to explore three Web pages of your own. The Web pages must all pertain to the same topic of your choice (examples: the Holocaust, gun control, AIDS, drug legalization). You will then rank the Web sites according to reliability and usefulness, applying all five criteria. You may use any search engine, directory, portal, or database to locate them. You may want to consider creating a *graphic organizer* or chart to help you rank your sites.

4. Your team will then give a fifteen- to twenty-minute presentation that will also include visuals, in either PowerPoint format, digital video, or photographs and posters. All team members should participate in the presentation and be prepared for questions or class discussion. You may want to review the *Rubrics* page to see exactly what's expected for your papers and presentation. Submit an outline or the presentation (if PowerPoint, iMovie, or Flash) upon completion of the project in person or via e-mail.

ASSESSMENT TIPS

- WebQuests should be accompanied by some form of an assessment rubric that lays out how each phase of the activity will be evaluated, along with both individual and group assessment.

- Students should be encouraged to assess not only their own participation in the quest, but also the resultant learning. Often the learning that comes from a WebQuest is extremely powerful for students. Consequently, they should have an opportunity to express that learning in an integrative and reflective paper or in some other fashion.

Final Thoughts on Collaborative Activities

The activities presented in this section demonstrate some of the more common uses of collaborative work. The ways collaboration can be used online are limitless: an instructor might create a game or use one that is available on the Internet, or the instructor might choose to modify any of the activities presented here. Anything that might serve the learning objectives of a particular course will work—creativity and imagination are the keys. We should never be afraid to try new and innovative ways of creating collaboration. Even if we fail, we learn from that failure, and that learning informs and enhances our teaching the next time around. What is important to remember in creating any collaborative activity is the process we discussed in Chapter Two:

- Set the stage.
- Create the environment.
- Model the process.
- Guide the process.
- Evaluate the process.

Regardless of the activity, if designed with this process in mind, the likelihood that students will engage with the activity successfully and experience minimal frustration increases. Collaborative activity does not give the instructor a "break" in his or her teaching schedule online. Instead, it provides a different and interesting way for students to engage with material and one another. A deeper and more satisfying learning process is the result.

SUMMARY POINTS TO REMEMBER ON COLLABORATIVE ACTIVITIES

- The collaborative activity chosen for a course should depend on the desired learning outcomes.

- The focus on outcomes can help to tease out whether to use one collaborative activity or another that is quite similar, such as deciding to use a role-playing activity or a simulation.

- Clear directions for completion of the activity should be provided to students at the start and the instructor should be available to guide the process throughout.

- Assessment of the activities should involve reflections on the activity itself, what students learned from doing it, and their thoughts about the contributions they themselves made, along with the contributions of others.

- Learning cycles are a good way to include multiple forms of team activity over a term or a period of weeks. They help to scaffold learning and the acquisition of knowledge and move students toward a final group project while keeping the same focus throughout, thus minimizing confusion or the need to reorganize the group for further activity.

Additional Resources

SIMULATIONS

The following resource is devoted to the design of computer simulations:

Aldrich, C. *Simulations and the Future of Learning: An Innovative (and Perhaps Revolutionary) Approach to e-Learning.* San Francisco: Pfeiffer, 2003.

CASE STUDIES

Numerous Internet sites provide case study material that can be integrated into an online course. Some of them are listed here:

Science Cases: http://ublib.buffalo.edu/libraries/projects/cases/ideas.htm

Economics Cases: http://www.unc.edu/home/pconway/aea2000/casesour.htm

Higher Education and Leadership: Harvard's Institutes of Higher Education, http://www.gse.harvard.edu/~ppe/highered/case.html

Various Content Areas: http://www.stolaf.edu/people/schodt/casebib.htm

http://www.merlot.org

The following books are also useful in working with case studies:

Honan, J. P., and Sternman Rule, C. *Using Cases in Higher Education.* San Francisco: Jossey-Bass, 2002.

Honan, J. P., and Sternman Rule, C. (eds.). *Casebook I: Faculty Employment Policies.* San Francisco: Jossey-Bass, 2002.

Honan, J. P., Sternman Rule, C., and Kenyon, S. B. *Teaching Notes to Casebook I.* San Francisco: Jossey-Bass, 2002.

BLOGS

The following sites can help increase knowledge about what a blog is and how it can be used:

http://www.blogger.com/about.pyra

http://www.rebeccablood.net/handbook/

WEBQUESTS

The following site provides information on creating Web quests as well as numerous examples created and submitted by others for review and use:

http://www.webquest.org

GAMES

There are numerous sites where collaborative games can be played. Here are two:

http://www.cranium.com/home.asp

http://www.cg.tuwien.ac.at/research/vr/gaming/

ADDING INTERACTIVITY TO COURSES

The following is a good source for interactive elements to add to courses; many of the elements can be used collaboratively:

http://www.alleni.com/home.asp

GRADING AND ASSESSMENT

The following book is an essential resource on the topic of assessment and grading:

Walvoord, B., *Effective Grading: A Tool for Learning and Assessment.* San Francisco: Jossey-Bass, 1998.

References

Angelo, T., and Cross, K. P. *Classroom Assessment Techniques.* San Francisco: Jossey-Bass, 1993.

Bailey, M. L., and Luetkehans, L. "Ten Great Tips for Facilitating Virtual Learning Teams." *Distance Learning '98: Proceedings of the Annual Conference on Distance Teaching and Learning.* Madison, Wis., August 5–7, 1998. (ED-422 838)

Blood, R. *The Weblog Handbook.* Boulder, Colo.: Perseus, 2002, http://www.rebeccablood. net/handbook/. Retrieved April 26, 2004.

Borden, L. M., and Perkins, D. F. "Assessing Your Collaboration: A Self Evaluation Tool." *Journal of Extension,* April 1999, *37*(2), http://joe.org/joe/1999april/tt1.html. Retrieved April 26, 2004.

Brookfield, S. D. *Developing Critical Thinkers: Challenging Adults to Explore Alternative Ways of Thinking and Acting.* San Francisco: Jossey-Bass, 1987.

Brookfield, S. D. *Becoming a Critically Reflective Teacher.* San Francisco: Jossey-Bass, 1995.

Brookfield, S. D., and Preskill, S. *Discussion as a Way of Teaching.* San Francisco: Jossey-Bass, 1999.

Byers, C. "Interactive Assessment and Course Transformation Using Web-Based Tools." *The Technology Source,* May/June 2002, http://ts.mivu.org/default.asp?show=article&id=928. Retrieved April 26, 2004.

Cashman, K. *Leadership from the Inside Out.* Provo, Utah: Executive Excellence, 1998.

Conrad, R. M., and Donaldson, A. *Engaging the Online Learner: Activities and Resources for Creative Instruction.* San Francisco: Jossey-Bass, 2004.

Davis, A. *Arizona Non-Profit Collaboration Manual.* PARTNERS, Inc., 1997, http://www. azpartners.org/collaborationManual.asp. Retrieved May 5, 2004.

Dell, D. "Philosophy of Online Teaching." Unpublished paper. Capella University, April 2004.

Doran, C. "The Effective Use of Learning Groups in Online Education." *New Horizons in Adult Education,* Summer 2001, *15*(2), http://www.nova.edu/~aed/horizons/volume15n2.html. Retrieved May 6, 2004.

Duarte, D., and Snyder, N. T. *Mastering Virtual Teams: Strategies, Tools, and Techniques that Succeed* (2nd ed.) San Francisco: Jossey-Bass, 2001.

DuPraw, M., and Axner, M. "Working on Common Cross-Cultural Communication Challenges." *AMPU Guide,* 1997, http://www.wwcd.org/action/ampu/crosscult.html. Retrieved May 5, 2004.

Ge, X., Yamashiro, K. A., and Lee, J. "Pre-Class Planning to Scaffold Students for Online Collaborative Learning Activities." *Educational Technology & Society,* July 2000, *3*(3), http://ifets.ieee.org/periodical/vol_3_2000/b02.html. Retrieved May 1, 2004.

Gunawardena, C. L., and Zittle, F. J. "Social Presence as a Predictor of Satisfaction with a Computer-Mediated Conferencing Environment." *American Journal of Distance Education,* 1997, *11*(3), 8–26.

Johnson, D., and Johnson, F. *Joining Together: Group Theory and Group Skills.* Needham Heights, Mass.: Allyn and Bacon, 2000.

Jonassen, D., and others. "Constructivism and Computer-Mediated Communication in Distance Education." *The American Journal of Distance Education,* 1995, *9*(2), 7–26.

Joo, J. "Cultural Issues of the Internet in Classrooms." *British Journal of Educational Technology,* July 1999, *30*(3), 245–250.

Kagan, S. *Cooperative Learning.* San Clemente, Calif.: Kagan, 1994.

Kazmer, M. M. "Coping in a Distance Environment: Sitcoms, Chocolate Cake, and Dinner with a Friend." *First Monday,* August 29, 2000, http://www.firstmonday.dk/issues/issue5_9/kazmer/index.html. Retrieved April 6, 2004.

Ko, S., and Rossen, S. *Teaching Online—A Practical Guide.* Boston: Houghton Mifflin, 2001.

McClure, B. *Putting a New Spin on Groups.* Hillsdale, N.J.: Erlbaum, 1998.

McGrath, J., and Hollingshead, A. *Groups Interacting with Technology.* Thousand Oaks, Calif.: Sage, 1994.

Millis, B. J. "Managing—and Motivating! Distance Learning Group Activities." (n.d.), http://www.tltgroup.org/gilbert/millis.htm. Retrieved April 6, 2004.

Morgan, C., and O'Reilly, M. *Assessing Open and Distance Learners.* London: Kogan Page, 1999.

Murphy, K., Drabier, R., and Epps, M. "Interaction and Collaboration via Computer Conferencing." *Proceedings of the National Convention for Education Communication and Technology,* 1998. (ED 423 852)

Palloff, R., and Pratt, K. *Building Learning Communities in Cyberspace: Effective Strategies for the Online Classroom.* San Francisco: Jossey-Bass, 1999.

Palloff, R., and Pratt, K. *Lessons from the Cyberspace Classroom: The Realities of Online Teaching.* San Francisco: Jossey-Bass, 2001.

Palloff, R., and Pratt, K. *The Virtual Student: A Profile and Guide to Working with Online Learners.* San Francisco: Jossey-Bass, 2003.

Piaget, J. *The Mechanisms of Perception.* New York: Routledge Kegan Paul, 1969.

Picciano, A. G. "Beyond Student Perception: Issues of Interaction, Presence, and Performance in an Online Course." *Journal of Asynchronous Learning Networks,* 2002, *6*(1), 21–40.

Preece, J. *Online Communities.* New York: Wiley, 2000.

Ragoonaden, K., and Bordeleau, B. "Collaborative Learning via the Internet." *Educational Technology & Society,* July 2000, *3*(3), http://ifets.ieee.org/periodical/vol_3_2000/b02.html. Retrieved May 1, 2004.

Shopler, J., Abell, M., and Galinsky, M. "Technology-Based Groups: A Review and Conceptual Framework for Practice." *Social Work,* May 1998, *4*(3), 254–269.

Sproull, L., and Kiesler, S. *Connections: New Ways of Working in the Networked Organization.* Boston: MIT Press, 1992.

Srinivas, H. "What is Collaborative Learning?" http://www.gdrc.org/kmgmt/c-learn/what-is-cl.html. Retrieved April 6, 2004.

Styers, A. Unpublished comprehensive paper. Capella University, April 2004.

Tu, C., and Corry, M. "Research in Online Learning Community," http://www.usq.edu.au/electpub/e-jist/docs/html2002/pdf/chtu.pdf, 2002. Retrieved April 6, 2004.

Tuckman, B., and Jensen, M. "Stages of Small Group Development Revisited." *Group and Organizational Studies,* 1977, *2*(4), 419–427.

Index